The CAST IRON Gourmet

CAMP CHEF
THE WAY TO COOK OUTDOORS

The CAST IRON
Gourmet

MATT PELTON

ISBN 13: 978-1-59955-370-2

Published by Hobble Creek Press, an imprint of Cedar Fort, Inc.

2373 W. 700 S., Springville, UT, 84663

Distributed by Cedar Fort, Inc., www.cedarfort.com

LIBRARY OF CONGRESS CATALOGING-IN-PUBLICATION DATA ON FILE

Cover and page design by Erica Dixon

Cover design © 2013 by Lyle Mortimer

Edited and typeset by Casey J. Winters

Printed in China

10 9 8 7 6 5 4 3 2 1

To my wife, Katie, who has helped me live my dreams for fifteen years.
I love you and appreciate all your support.

Table of CONTENTS

PREFACE

MY EARLIEST MEMORIES of food almost always center around cast iron. Starting at around the age of eight, I would take to the fields near my house and start a fire to cook in a cast-iron pan. I would oftentimes sneak a package of deer steaks out of the freezer, and my friends and siblings would gather around to eat my creations. But sometimes my creations were terrible! I tried cooking a pizza once, and the recipe called for a package of yeast in the dough. I did not know at the time that a package was a unit of measurement and not a physical package. I did as the recipe suggested and added the "package" of yeast. The pizza was a disaster to say the least, more of a yeasty calzone as the doughy mass enveloped the sauce and toppings, trapping them inside.

As time went on I became better at the art, but one thing remained constant: cooking outdoors with cast-iron cookware. In the town I grew up in, in central Utah, rarely did an outdoor activity not include something cooked in a Dutch oven. At Scout camp, a Dutch oven was a staple, whether it be a chicken in mushroom gravy or a 7Up cobbler. In the darkness of the Scout camp, we would remove the coals and blow off the ashes to be rewarded with the smells of perceived culinary perfection. When I was fourteen years old, I had convinced my parents to let me and a friend miss three days of school to go elk hunting. Our dads had to work but would be up on Friday night to hunt with us. By this time, I had gained a small reputation of being a decent cook with a Dutch oven. We had loaded for bear with all the wonderful foods we were going to make at elk camp: sourdough starter for bread and pancakes, potatoes and sausage for mountain man breakfast, and hunks of elk meat from the year before for dinners. What we ate in reality was a much different story. Morning came and we were so busy saddling horses and getting gear together before light that the pancakes and mountain man breakfasts were set aside for granola bars and a swig of orange juice. Lunchtimes were spent on the mountain eating squished peanut butter and jelly sandwiches and fruit we shared with the horses.

After dark we returned to camp and lacked the energy to cook, so we settled for opening cold cans of beef stew and eating them straight from the can. Friday night came, and my friend and I were on top of the mountain above camp at least a two-mile ride and a thousand vertical feet. The sun was beginning to set and the elk were beginning to move when through the smell of the pines wafted one of the most tantalizing smells I had experienced at that time in my life. The smell of home-cooked rolls and chili cooked in the Dutch oven wafted up to our noses, and all thoughts of hunting left as our hungry stomachs took over. We saddled the horses as fast as we could and rode down the mountain to camp. As we rode into camp, my dad and my friend's dad were setting the table and removing the coals from the Dutch ovens. They had cooked one of the best meals I have eaten in my life, possibly because my friend and I were on the brink of starvation.

Dutch ovens became such a part of my life that I packed a ten-inch Dutch oven in my luggage when I left home at nineteen to serve a two-year LDS mission to Boston. While on the East Coast, I learned how to cook meals from many different cultures and incorporate them into my meals and menus. After returning home, I took my passion to a whole new level and started to cook gourmet and eventually started entering Dutch oven and barbecue competitions. In March of 2012, I took the title of Dutch oven world champion with my friend and cooking partner, Doug Martin.

Throughout the book, I hope to share with you the passion I feel about Dutch oven cooking and share tips and techniques that I have learned from years of trial and error. The recipes included are tried and true, with easy-to-follow instructions and prep times that will make them a joy to cook. Enjoy!

Chapter ONE

BUYING
A DUTCH OVEN

I DON'T REMEMBER WHAT my first Dutch oven was or where it came from. I wish I still had it. I don't know if it had a brand name or if it was old or relatively new. The one thing I do remember is how well it cooked. It was a twelve-inch Dutch oven and could accommodate feeding two people all the way up to a dozen without difficulty. I cooked many different items in that pot, from cobblers to lasagna, and they all tasted great. When I went on my mission, I specifically remember that the ten-inch Dutch oven I brought with me was a no-name brand. It had a great seasoning on it and a tight-fitting lid. It wasn't until I became much older that I became more brand specific—and for several reasons. First and foremost is the importance of quality cast iron. Some cast has a rougher surface than others, and the "tolerances" are not as tight. "Tolerance" is how tight the lid fits to the pot: When you look at the gap between the lid and the pot, you should not see more than ⅛ inch of space. If you move the lid from side to side while on the pot, you should not be able to move it farther than ¼ inch. Any more than that and the Dutch oven will not seal properly and cook the way you want it to.

In my opinion, the Camp Chef and Lodge brands are the very best for the nationally available Dutch ovens. Both companies have strict quality control and put out a great product. If I were to give one brand an edge, I would give it to Camp Chef. The Lodge has tighter tolerances because of the casting process, but the Camp Chef has the better designs, cooks just as well, and costs less. One of my favorite features in the Camp Chef ovens is the thermometer port cast into the iron.

What size of Dutch oven should I get?

The answer to this depends on what you are going to use it for. Is this your first Dutch oven? Are you going to use it mainly outdoors or indoors? You can find so many types, styles, and sizes on the market.

I have found that the very best Dutch oven to start with is a twelve-inch oven, for several reasons: almost all Dutch oven recipe books have recipes designed for a twelve-inch oven; a twelve-inch is small enough to cook for two but large enough to cook for twelve; and the twelve-inch is the most versatile, allowing you to cook everything from stews to cakes.

My second choice is the ten-inch Dutch oven. My favorite ten-inch is the Whitetail oven from Camp Chef. I use this Dutch oven more than all my other ovens combined. The ten-inch is great because most of your recipes work for them as well, but they are lighter weight and oftentimes I don't need the extra cooking room unless I am catering an event. I cook a lot of cakes in the Dutch oven, and the ten-inch is my absolute favorite because I can drop the cakes out of the pan and design them with little or no trimming. I own a selection of fourteen-inch Dutch ovens, and I use them regularly, but they are specialized. I use a fourteen-inch, Camp Chef Lewis and Clark Dutch oven as a steam oven for cooking artisan breads. I use some Camp Chef Ultimate, fourteen-inch Dutch ovens for steaming and smoking. The only other time I use them is on the occasion that I need to cook a one-pot meal for a large group. I have some sixteen-inch Dutch ovens—the Grizzly from Camp Chef, for example—but I don't use them as often as my smaller Dutch ovens. Any Dutch oven over sixteen inches is a waste of time and money in my opinion. I bought a twenty-four-inch Dutch oven at a rendezvous at Fort Bridger once, thinking it was the end-all of all Dutch ovens. On its maiden voyage I cooked ham and twenty dozen eggs to make a breakfast for the whole camp. I had at least two problems: it was too large to distribute the heat evenly, and it took a minimum of three men to carry the stupid thing. I think Dutch ovens of that size are only good for two things: flower pots and boat anchors.

Should I buy cast iron or aluminum?

Cast iron really is what Dutch ovens are all about. The only time I would recommend an aluminum Dutch oven is if you are traveling somewhere and need to conserve on weight. In that instance, an aluminum Dutch oven is better than no Dutch oven at all. Aluminum has two advantages: weight and ease of cleaning. The advantages of cast iron over aluminum, however, are far greater:

1. Cast iron is a healthy way to cook. In a study conducted by the FDA they found that 70 percent of Americans are anemic to some degree. We simply don't get enough iron in our diet. We are told that red meat and dark greens are the best food sources for iron, but what they don't tell you is that those sources are not soluble, and your body only uses a small percentage of the iron. However, the iron in cast iron is soluble and cooks into your food; your body will use 80 percent of this iron.

2. The patina on cast iron is Mother Nature's Teflon because it is made of pure carbon, binding to the cast iron. Teflon is a carcinogen when heated up to six hundred degrees.

Your home stove can reach that temperature easily. When Teflon starts to chip and flake, the pan is only good for the garbage because it is dangerous to cook with. Dutch ovens build up a nice black layer of carbon over time called patina. Patina will create a smooth, nonstick surface that is completely safe and natural.

3. Cast iron distributes and holds heat better than other options. The pores in cast iron fill up with oil and allow the heat to transfer better throughout the pot. Once cast iron is hot, it takes a long time to cool down, keeping your food nice and warm until you are ready to eat it.

Should I buy preseasoned or raw cast iron?

This should not be too much of a question anymore because raw cast iron is very hard to find now. Most manufacturers are doing the initial seasoning for you, and their Dutch ovens are ready to cook right out of the box. This costs a little bit more but is well worth the price when you consider all that is involved in taking raw iron and turning it into a black pot.

Should I buy an in-home or outdoor model?

I have many of both of these, but my in-home model sees far more use than my outdoor models. Where are you going to cook with it the most? I cook several days a week in mine and do not usually have the time to start coals to cook dinner. The in-home models do not have legs and have a domed lid. They can be used on the stovetop to stew or in the oven to bake or roast. Camping or outdoor models have legs and a flat lid with a rim on them to hold the oven off the coals and hold coals on the top.

• RECAP •

The following are things to consider for your first Dutch oven:

Buy a ten- or twelve-inch Dutch oven. • Buy cast iron unless you need less weight.
Buy a preseasoned model. • Decide if you are going to use it in-home or outdoors.

Chapter TWO

TOOLS
FOR THE DUTCH OVEN

WHEN I WAS A TEENAGER, I decided to cook an elk roast in the Dutch oven outside. My parents were gone and I was cooking dinner for my siblings. I started it off with a thawed elk roast, seasonings, water, onions, and potatoes. I fired up some coals and set it up on the concrete behind the house. After three hours of roasting, it was time to check the dinner. I had not thought this through very well; I did not know how I was going to take the lid off. I tried some pliers, but when I lifted the lid, some of the ashes fell into the pot as the lid clumsily tipped and swayed. I inspected the food and searched for another way to lift the lid. I settled on an old claw hammer and placed the claw under the hook and lifted it with much more success. I used that old claw hammer for years cooking Dutch, and it worked fine. When I was in metal shop in high school, one of my first projects was to build a lid lifter. I built it out of rebar, and with a little bending and welding, I had a heck of a lid lifter. I used an old stove shovel to place the coals around the Dutch oven and lid. I used a piece of plate from metal shop to cook on so I didn't destroy the concrete and lose half of my heat. This was a crude setup, but it worked well for years. Nowadays there is no end to the tools available to help you in your Dutch oven cooking pursuits.

What tools do I need to get started?

Once you have your Dutch oven, I would suggest a nice lid lifter that will allow you to lift the lid and dump the coals off. Several lifters are on the market, but I am fond of a new one made by Camp Chef: it is well balanced and versatile. You will also need a pair of tongs and a shovel for placing and removing coals. You can retire a sturdy pair of metal kitchen tongs or buy some from any manufacturer of outdoor cooking equipment. Once you have all these things, you are ready to cook! I will mention other tools here that will make your life easier but are not necessary.

DUTCH OVEN TABLE: These are great because they elevate your food so you don't have to cook at ground level. Nowadays I am lost without my two Camp Chef Dutch oven tables. They also allow you to cook almost anywhere without fear of burning up grass or staining sidewalks. Cleanup is easy, and most models come with a wind screen to help your coals from burning out.

CHARCOAL-LIGHTING BASKET: This is another tool I would have a hard time giving back! It is so easy to wrinkle up some paper, place it in the bottom, and light it—no fuel, no fuss. Weber and Camp Chef both make fantastic, inexpensive models. I like the Camp Chef model because it is the largest and lights the coals quicker.

DUTCH OVEN DOME: I love this product, also made by Camp Chef. It can increase cooking times as well as insulate from bad weather. It was designed so you can bake on a propane stovetop, and with its diffuser plate, it works quite well.

DUTCH OVEN BAGS: These are nice because they keep your Dutch ovens from getting dirty. When I was young, the back of the truck always had hay and dirt in it. After I took the Dutch ovens camping, they would be covered in hay, and oftentimes I had difficulty cleaning off the lids. Camp Chef makes a one-size-fits-most bag.

TRIVETS: Build or buy a few trivets to keep around. Trivets are nice to set your lid on when you are checking the food. They will also keep you from burning tables with a hot Dutch oven full of food.

PAN SCRAPERS: These are small plastic squares of different sizes to fit different pans. They are made by Camp Chef and cost a couple of dollars each.

Chapter THREE

SEASONING
YOUR DUTCH OVEN

I HAD SOMEONE tell me once that his Dutch oven was so well seasoned that he didn't have to use any spices to cook his food. Yuck. He didn't understand the meaning of seasoning in Dutch oven terms. You don't want your chocolate cake to taste like lasagna, that's for sure. When I was young, I didn't fully understand what seasoning was either. I knew it was the black stuff on the pan and that the blacker the pan the better.

To understand seasoning, you need to understand cast iron. Cast iron is full of small pits and fissures. Seasoning is filling those pits and fissures with oil and patina. It's as simple as that. I had a neighbor who brought me some of her grandmother's skillets, saying that they needed to be reseasoned. One look at them and I gave them back to her, saying that my only hope is to have beautiful pans like that someday. The patina was so thick that it was mirror-smooth and glossy. Oftentimes I hear that someone has an old Dutch oven that cooks better than any new Dutch oven. That's fairly true if the Dutch oven has been taken care of properly. The more you use your Dutch oven, the more patina you build up. The more patina you build up, the better your pan will cook.

Almost all Dutch ovens now come preseasoned and ready to cook. You can tell immediately: if the pot is black, it's preseasoned. If you buy a raw Dutch oven or find a rusted out one, they will need to be seasoned.

How do I season my Dutch oven?

If you have a raw cast oven, you will need to remove the packaging grease first. Manufacturers will coat the cast iron in mineral oil to prevent the metal from rusting until the consumer buys it. To remove the packaging grease, heat up the Dutch oven on a stovetop and wipe away as much grease as you can. When the Dutch oven starts to cool down but is still warm, wash it well with dish soap and a scrub brush. Scrub it hard and rinse it well.

If you have an old and rusty Dutch oven, the process is similar. Heat the Dutch oven on a stovetop and wipe it out using vegetable oil until the rust is gone. (If the rust is deep, you can soak it overnight in a cola to help clean and remove the rust.) Once the rust is gone, wash the Dutch oven well using dish soap while the pan is still warm. After you are done washing the pan, wipe the water out with a paper towel and let it air-dry for a while. When the pan is dry, heat it up again and rub Camp Chef Cast Iron Conditioner or canola oil on all surfaces of the Dutch oven. Preheat your oven or outside grill to five hundred degrees and place the pan in upside down and the lid right side up on top of the inverted Dutch oven legs. When the oil vaporizes at around four hundred degrees, it will rise. If your pan is not upside down, the oil will rise and stick onto something other than your Dutch oven. As the oil vaporizes, it will be drawn into the pits and fissures of the Dutch oven. When the oil eventually burns, it will smoke, and the residual oil will turn to carbon and bind with the cast iron, turning to patina. You want to keep your Dutch ovens in the oven or outside grill until they stop smoking. If you do this in the house, be sure to have the windows open and the fans on. This is also a good time to practice fire drills with your family because the house will be filled with smoke and the detectors will be going crazy. I know; I speak from experience. When the Dutch oven stops smoking, remove it from the oven and wipe it down with the conditioner again. If you see spots that are still gray, put the Dutch oven back into the oven until it is completely black. Once the Dutch oven has cooled, wipe out any excess oil.

The Dutch oven is now ready to cook in. Patina will build up over time. The more you cook, the more carbon will build up from your food and bind to the existing patina. The more often you use your pan, the smoother the surface will become and the better it will cook.

How do I reseason my Dutch oven?

I like to reseason my Dutch ovens about once a year and always before a competition. Without regular seasoning, the Dutch ovens will become dry, food will stick, and the heat won't be as even in the pan. Lewis and Clark in their expedition out West specifically wrote that they were excited to shoot a bear because now they had fat to season their Dutch ovens. To reseason a Dutch oven, follow the instructions from above, though you don't have to soak in cola or scrub nearly as hard since you are building up what you have already established as a seasoning on your pot. You can reseason as often or as little as you like; the more you do it, the faster your Dutch oven will morph into one of the Dutch ovens of old and cook like a champ.

Will rust ruin my Dutch oven?

No, as long as it is not extensive. Cast iron is prone to rusting a small amount when moisture is introduced. If your Dutch oven has a little bit of rust in it, wipe it out with paper towels and canola oil multiple times, until the paper towels come out clean. If the rust is extensive, follow the instructions above and reseason the pan.

• RECAP •

To season a Dutch oven, follow these steps:

Clean and remove all packaging grease or rust. • Heat up Dutch oven and wipe it down with cast iron conditioner or canola oil. • Place in the oven or outdoor grill heated to five hundred degrees. • Make sure the Dutch oven is upside down and the lid right side up on top of legs. • Leave it in the oven until it stops smoking. • Remove Dutch oven from the grill or oven and wipe down all sides with cast iron conditioner or canola oil. • Let it cool down completely. • Wipe out any excess oil. • Repeat if necessary.

Chapter
FOUR

CLEANING
YOUR DUTCH OVEN

CLEANING IS ONE of the most misunderstood processes with Dutch oven cooking. When I was young, I tried everything told to me by friends, family, even books. I lined my Dutch ovens with foil to make cleanup easy, I scrubbed the Dutch ovens with salt, I burned them out with fire. I essentially did everything that was wrong and bad for the Dutch ovens. First, lining a Dutch oven with foil may make for an easier cleanup, but it will not cook like cast iron, and you will get hot spots in your pan. Also, if your foil tears and leaks, the food that gets between the cast iron and the foil will experience superheat, and the resulting mess is difficult to remove. Second, scrubbing a Dutch oven with salt is a bad idea all around. Salt is abrasive by nature and corrosive when it comes in contact with water. The salt will remove patina fast and get you back to raw cast iron. Any salt that is left behind will become corrosive when it comes in contact with the humidity in the air. The salt will eat into the patina and iron and ruin your Dutch oven. Third, burning out the food in a Dutch oven is probably the worst idea of them all.

A typical campfire will burn close to 1,300 degrees. That is hot enough to destroy the patina and warp the cast iron. Any food particles that do remain are now big clumps of carbon that are almost impossible to remove. When I cleaned this way, I started to see that I was damaging my Dutch ovens. I learned a little at a time the right way to clean a Dutch oven and where the wives' tales came from.

What is the best way to clean my Dutch oven?

First, cleaning when the pan is still warm is always easiest. Scrape out any remaining food with a pan scraper or spatula. Wipe out any sauce or residue with a paper towel. If you have a sink or running water available, scrub out the pan in the water and rinse well. If you cooked something acidic or especially oily, use a small amount of soap and scrub it out. Make sure to rinse the pan very well. After the pan is clean and rinsed, dry off with paper towels and make sure they are coming out clean—if not, keep cleaning. Let the Dutch oven air-dry or heat it slightly until it's completely dry. This method is very simple. However, if you're out camping and don't have running warm water, use a spray bottle with a four-to-one ratio of water and vinegar. First, scrape out the Dutch oven with a scraper. Wipe out the residual food and oil with a paper towel. Spray the vinegar and water and wipe out the Dutch oven. Continue spraying and wiping out the oven until the paper towels come out clean. Let the Dutch oven air-dry until it is completely dry.

I have heard to never use soap on cast iron; is that true?

This is one of the old wives' tales and something I bought into for a long time. You can use small amounts of soap to clean out cast iron, but follow a couple of rules:

1. MAKE SURE you have hot water. If your water is cold, the soap will stay on your Dutch oven and flavor your food with its essence. When the pan and water are hot, the pores will open and the soap can remove excess build up while not staying on the pan.

2. AVOID USING harsh, concentrated detergents. These soaps will wear down the patina and cause it to weaken its bond to the cast iron. If you have a concentrated dish detergent, dilute it with water before using it. I like to dilute it twenty-to-one and use it in a small bottle.

3. NEVER PUT a Dutch oven in the dishwasher; it will ruin the cast iron.

Can I use metal scrapers to clean out cast iron?

Yes, you can without too much of a problem. But be sure to use them flat against the surface. If you scrape with the edge of a metal tool, you can scratch the patina and cause damage to it. With plastic or wood, you never have this problem, but for me, wood harbors bacteria, and sometimes plastic is not strong enough. Remember, cast iron is iron and is pretty durable.

Desserts are always so hard to clean up after; how do I make it easier?

Cleaning up after cooking a cobbler is one of the reasons most people turn to foil, but it doesn't need to be that way. The sugars in a dessert can bind to the cast iron, making it difficult and tedious to clean. If you have it available, heat up some water to a boil, pour it in the Dutch oven, and let it sit for a few minutes. Then you can scrape or scrub the Dutch oven out with ease. I have made hundreds of desserts and never had a problem cleaning up after them using this method.

• RECAP •

To clean a Dutch oven follow these steps:

Make sure Dutch oven is warm. • Scrape out all food particles with a scraper. • Wipe out residual food or sauce. • Use light soap, warm water, and a scrub brush to scrub pan well (vinegar and water if no running water is available). • Wipe out the water with a paper towel and make sure it is clean. • Let the Dutch oven air dry or heat it until it is dry.

Chapter FIVE

STORING
YOUR DUTCH OVEN

SO MANY PEOPLE only use their Dutch ovens a couple of times a year for scout camp or elk camp in the fall. Some of us who constantly cook with Dutch ovens do not have to think a lot about longtime storage. When the Dutch oven comes out of storage, many people take off the lid to a rancid oil smell and a gray Dutch oven with little black flakes in the bottom. These people will wipe it out as best as they can, but the first meal will always taste a little like rank oil. (On a good note, at least the Dutch ovens were probably not rusty.) This is a problem with many Dutch oven owners, who don't know how to store their Dutch ovens properly. What happens is the oil comes in contact with humidity, goes rancid, and turns to acid; the acid eats at the patina, and the bad oil fills the pores of the Dutch oven.

How should I store my Dutch ovens?
Storing them dry with something between the lid and the pan works well. When

you're done using your Dutch oven, air-dry it for a while until you are sure it is completely dry. Do not wipe it down with oil! Place a piece of newspaper or paper towel between the lid and the pan and store it in a cool and dry place. If you have a Dutch oven case, use it to keep dust from settling on your Dutch oven. (Ideally, I would love to have a wire rack system to set all my Dutch ovens in the basement upside down with the lids sitting on top of the legs.) Dutch ovens get into trouble when the moisture from the air is trapped inside, which is why you need to keep a spacer between the lid and pan. Paper works really well because it wicks the moisture out of the pan. Don't worry about it rusting; if you're storing the Dutch oven in a dry spot, it shouldn't rust, and if it does, it will rust very little and will be easy to wipe out.

I stored my Dutch oven wrong, and now it is rancid; how do I fix it?

If this happens, you have one course of action. Follow the steps for seasoning a Dutch oven and completely reseason it. When you are done, you should not be able to smell any rancid oil: if you can still smell it, repeat the process until you no longer can.

Is there anything I need to do after storage before I use my Dutch oven?

When it's time to use your Dutch oven, open it up and inspect it well. If there is a little rust or dust, heat the oven up and wipe it out with oil. If it is clean and smells nice, wipe it down with a light coat of canola oil or Camp Chef Conditioner and you're ready to go.

Chapter SIX

COOKING
TECHNIQUES

I ALWAYS THOUGHT that because it's called a Dutch *oven*, I had to use it as an oven and only bake in it. No matter what I cooked, I faithfully put coals on top and bottom and went to town. If I cooked with more than one Dutch oven, I stacked them up and away I went. This method worked for the fact that the food cooked and tasted good, but problems arose. I burnt the bottoms of breads all the time and caramelized the tops of my chili pots, burning the beans. This handicap set me back for many years, thinking that some things couldn't be cooked in a Dutch oven. I know different now. If you can cook it, you can cook it in a Dutch oven. A lot of things are easier to cook in a Dutch oven because you can adjust your heat as needed. The following are four basic methods for cooking in a Dutch oven.

Stewing

This method is used to cook all soups, stews, chilis, and braised meat dishes. Stewing requires a checkerboard of charcoals on the bottom with no coals on the lid. With soups especially, any heat on the lid will cause a film to form on top of the soup or stew and burn the bigger parts that float to the top while cooking.

Roasting

This is the method for cooking whole meat dishes like loins, roasts, and whole chickens. To create a roasting pattern, place a checkerboard of charcoal on the bottom and a ring of coals on the top. As the heat in the bottom of the Dutch oven raises the temperature of the meat, the liquid cascades out of the meat and is caramelized. You are trying to create a convection of hot air in the Dutch oven—the unevenness of the top and bottom heat will cause the heat to move. You want to use very little if any liquid at all when roasting, otherwise you will braise it. A lot of people will buy a small, round cooling rack to lift the meat off the bottom. Others will place the meat on a bed of onions to accomplish the same thing. Whatever method you use, turn the meat over frequently so it will caramelize on all sides.

Baking

This is the method used for all baked goods, from dinner rolls to cakes and cobblers. It uses the same heat on all sides of the Dutch oven. To create a true baking oven, place a ring of charcoals on the bottom with the coals sticking halfway out so it will heat up the sides. Place a checkerboard of charcoals on the top. If you follow this method closely, you will rarely burn the bottom of anything.

Broiling

This method is used a lot as a stage in the cooking process but not usually by itself. I use this method to brown the top of a cobbler or bubble the cheese on a pizza or lasagna. Occasionally I will use this method to cook some steaks or salmon. To create a broil, all the heat has to come from above. To accomplish this, use a checkerboard pattern of coals on the top only.

How many coals do I need to use?

So many people get hung up about exact amounts of coals. The nice thing about Dutch oven cooking is that you do not need to have the exact amount of heat. Coals vary greatly from brand to brand; some brands burn hotter than others. The climate makes a big difference as well—coals burn hotter at lower elevations than at higher. If it is a cloudy, wet day, coals won't burn as hot as they will on a warm, sunny day. There is just no way to accurately give you a graph to tell you how many coals to use. The more important thing is how the coals are placed rather than the amount of coals. The other thing to understand is that coals cook by heating up the air around them rather than by direct conduction. If you leave at least an inch of space around each coal, you will get more heat than if you place them on top of each other. If you use the inch or so of space, generally the Dutch oven will hold about as many coals as needed. For example, a ten-inch Dutch oven will hold the right amount of coals if they are spaced properly. The same goes for a twelve- or fourteen-inch. The nice thing is Dutch ovens are very forgiving and will still cook well with a large variance in temperature. If it's a little cool, it will take longer to cook than if it's hot. Therefore, use the coal patterns and spacing rather than counting out individual coals. The basic rule of thumb is that one charcoal will equal approximately thirteen degrees of heat inside your Dutch Oven.

Can I cook with my Dutch oven inside?

You can, but you are limited to baking and stewing only. You can put your Dutch oven inside your conventional oven and bake; simply add twenty-five degrees to the desired heat in the recipe. You'll have no problems cooking on the stovetop, but be careful with a glass-top stove because the legs can scratch the glass. In this situation, buying a home model Dutch oven would be better for you.

Chapter SEVEN

BREAKFAST

BREAKFAST RECIPES are some of my favorite recipes to make in a Dutch oven. There is nothing more nostalgic for me than waking up to the smell of a mountain man breakfast or sourdough pancakes slowly cooking on cast iron. I hope you enjoy these recipes as much as I have over the years.

Method
Roasting

Completion Time
Less than 1 hour

Dutch Oven Placement
12-inch Dutch oven
Approximately 8 coals top
and 10 coals bottom

TOP PLACEMENT

BOTTOM PLACEMENT

Mountain Man BREAKFAST

THIS IS ONE of my all-time favorite breakfasts because it is easy to make, very filling, and tastes so good. This recipe will feed about ten people, so adjust it accordingly. It can be served as a stand-alone meal or put into flour tortillas for an amazing breakfast burrito.

1 Tbsp. oil

1 lb. small diced potatoes, potato tots, or Southern-style hash browns

1 lb. breakfast sausage, diced ham, or chopped bacon

1 dozen eggs

½ lb. shredded cheddar cheese

1 (4-oz.) can diced jalapeños or green chilies (optional; if you want it slightly milder)

Salt and pepper to taste

To begin, heat up a little oil in the bottom of the Dutch oven. When the oil gets hot and starts to separate, stir in the potatoes and scrape the bottom until they start to brown slightly. Add the sausage. Cover the Dutch oven and place coals on the top and roast for 15 minutes, stirring it once in that time. Remove the Dutch oven from the heat and fold in the eggs. Add the cheese and optional chilies and stir them in. Cover the Dutch oven and let it sit for five minutes without any heat. Serve.

AT HOME: Use your range top on medium heat and cover the Dutch oven when you aren't actively stirring the dish. The recipe will take a little bit longer.

Best Scones EVER

A T HOME I make these scones almost every other week. They are very easy to make, and they are so good. The outside is crispy and flaky with a marshmallow-soft inside that dissolves in your mouth. Slathered in honey butter, these scones will remind you of a time past.

FOR THE SCONE DOUGH:

Use the Basic White Bread recipe on page 50.

FOR THE HONEY BUTTER:

1 stick butter, softened   1 pinch salt

3 Tbsp. honey

 Begin by kneading the bread dough; it should be somewhat sticky but still able workable. Pinch off into golf ball–sized chunks and lay out on a greased cookie sheet. Cover the cookie sheet with plastic wrap and let dough balls rise for about an hour. Fill 10-inch Dutch oven a quarter full with canola oil. Set the Dutch oven on the coals for 10 minutes or until the oil sizzles when you put a small drop of water in it. Take the scones one at a time and stretch them thin. Carefully let them slide into the oil. Turn when the edges start to look gold. Remove from the oil and pat dry with a paper towel. For the honey butter, set the butter out until it's soft. Fold and whip the butter until it's smooth. Fold in the honey a little at a time, followed by the salt.

AT HOME: Use the Dutch oven on the range top set to medium-high.

Method
Stewing

Completion Time
2 hours

Dutch Oven Placement
10-inch Dutch oven
Approximately 14 coals
on the bottom

TOP
PLACEMENT

BOTTOM
PLACEMENT

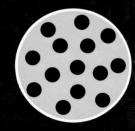

Method
Stewing

Completion Time
Overnight prep
30 minutes to prepare and cook

Dutch Oven Placement
12-inch cast-iron skillet
Approximately 12 coals on
the bottom

TOP PLACEMENT

BOTTOM PLACEMENT

Dad's Sourdough PANCAKES

WHEN I WAS growing up, this was my favorite breakfast ever. My dad would cook these religiously every weekend when he wasn't working. We often had homemade chokecherry or elderberry syrup to put on top. I liked to slather the pancakes in butter and taste the unique flavor of the sourdough. This recipe will feed six to eight people.

FOR THE STARTER:

2 cups warm water

2 tsp. yeast

½ cup sugar

2 tsp. salt

2 cups flour

FOR THE BATTER:

1½ cups milk

⅓ cup sugar

2 tsp. salt

1 tsp. vanilla

2 tsp. baking powder

3 eggs

2–3 cups flour, depending on the thickness of the batter

The night before, mix up the starter ingredients in a bowl and cover. In the morning, mix in the batter ingredients—use only 2 cups of flour at first and add more if needed to have the consistency of batter you desire. Always cook a test pancake first and adjust the batter using milk to thin it or flour to thicken it. Place the 12-inch skillet on a trivet with coals underneath.

Place 4 coals underneath a Dutch oven, hanging halfway out the side. When you have a pancake done, place it in the Dutch oven and put the lid back on. This will keep all the pancakes warm until they are ready to eat.

 AT HOME: Use your skillet on the stovetop. Place pancakes in some foil to keep them warm until done.

Method
Baking

Completion Time
45 minutes

Dutch Oven Placement
12-inch Dutch oven
Approximately 12 coals on
top and 8 coals on bottom

TOP PLACEMENT

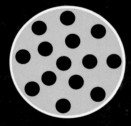

BOTTOM PLACEMENT

German PANCAKES

I LEARNED TO make these when I was living on the East Coast. They are a wonderful, fluffy egg dish that is fabulous when drizzled with powdered sugar and fruit or even plain maple syrup. The best thing is that they are incredibly easy to make.

½ stick butter

1 cup flour

1 cup milk

6 eggs

1 tsp. salt

1 tsp. vanilla

2 tsp. baking powder

 Mix all the ingredients well in a bowl. Pour into a warm, well-greased Dutch oven. Bake for 40 minutes or until the top is golden and a knife will come out clean in the center. Slice it into chunks, add your topping of choice, and enjoy.

AT HOME: Place the Dutch in a 350-degree oven. Do not use the lid. Remove when the top is browning.

Huevos RANCHEROS

THIS SOUTH-OF-THE-BORDER classic breakfast is a crowd pleaser. It's easy to make and goes well with any outdoor activity. Serve this with either flour or corn tortillas heated up for some amazing breakfast burritos.

1 Tbsp. oil

½ ring smoked sausage (Hill-shire Farms or similar), chopped

2 Roma tomatoes, diced

½ (14-oz.) can black beans, rinsed

1 (7-oz.) can salsa verde (I prefer the Herdez brand)

1 dozen eggs

8 oz. shredded jack cheese or Mexican blend

1 avocado, chopped (optional)

Flour or corn tortillas, heated (I prefer corn, lightly fried in oil)

Sour cream (optional)

Cilantro (optional)

 Start by placing a lightly oiled Dutch oven on a checkerboard of coals. Stir in the sausage chunks and cook them until they start to brown. Add the Roma tomatoes, black beans, and salsa. Stir them in. Cover and roast for 10–15 minutes. Remove the Dutch oven from the heat and stir in the eggs. Cover and let it sit for 5 minutes. Stir the mixture well. Add the cheese and fold it in. Return to heat and fold until the eggs are set. Fold in the optional avocados and serve on tortillas. Garnish with the sour cream and cilantro.

AT HOME: Cook this on your range top turned to medium heat. Use the lid as often as possible. It will take a little longer.

Method
Roasting

Completion Time
45 minutes

Dutch Oven Placement
12-inch Dutch oven
Approximately 10 coals on top and 14 on the bottom

TOP PLACEMENT

BOTTOM PLACEMENT

Method
Roasting

Completion Time
Less than 30 minutes

Dutch Oven Placement
**10-inch Dutch oven
Approximately 6 coals on
top and 10 coals on bottom**

TOP PLACEMENT

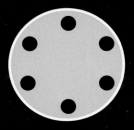

BOTTOM PLACEMENT

California OMELETS

I LOVE OMELETS, and a 10-inch Dutch oven is the perfect omelet maker. This recipe is one of my favorites. The trick is in the folding—it may take a couple of times before you get it down. Once you figure out how to fold, however, it will be second nature. This omelet will usually feed two people.

1 Tbsp. oil

4 large eggs

Tony Chachere's Creole Seasoning or similar spice to taste

2 oz. sliced turkey

2 oz. cream cheese, cut into strips

2 oz. shredded cheddar cheese

½ avocado, sliced

Begin by placing your coals underneath your Dutch oven in a checkerboard pattern, leaving 2 inches of space between the coals. Add a small amount of oil to the bottom of the Dutch oven. Mix the eggs in a bowl, adding the Creole seasoning. Pour slowly into the Dutch oven. Cover the Dutch oven and place a few coals in a ring pattern on the lid. Cook for 3 minutes and remove the lid. Add the turkey followed by the cheeses and the avocado. Cover and cook for 2 minutes. Remove the lid. The eggs should be mostly set by this time. Tip the Dutch oven to a 45-degree angle and then slide your spatula under one half of the omelet and fold it over. Remove the Dutch oven from the heat and let it sit for 5 minutes. Remove omelets and serve.

AT HOME: Use your range top set to medium-low. Make sure to use the lid on the Dutch oven.

Philly Cheesesteak OMELETS

THIS IS ONE OF MY FAVORITE omelet recipes if I have leftover steak from the night before. You can also use this recipe and technique for a Denver Omelet—simply replace the steak with ham and the cream cheese with cheddar cheese.

1 Tbsp. oil

1 oz. sliced bell pepper (I prefer red)

1 oz. thinly sliced onion

1 oz. sliced mushroom (I prefer brown)

4 oz. cooked steak, cut into strips

4 large eggs

Tony Chachere's Creole Seasoning or similar spice to taste

2 oz. cream cheese, cut into strips

Begin by placing the coals underneath your Dutch oven in a checkerboard pattern, leaving 2 inches of space between the coals. Add a small amount of oil to the bottom of the Dutch oven. In a skillet, sauté the peppers, onions, and mushrooms until the onions are clear and the peppers are beginning to brown. Add the steak strips and remove the Dutch oven from the heat: the residual heat of the Dutch oven will finish cooking the steak. (I leave the Dutch oven on the coals just long enough to stir in the steak and for the meat to start browning on the edges.) Mix the eggs in a bowl, adding the Creole seasoning. Pour slowly into the Dutch oven. Cover the Dutch oven and place a few coals in a ring pattern on the lid. Cook for 3 minutes and remove the lid. Add the steak, peppers, onions, and mushrooms, followed by the cream cheese. Cover and cook for 2 minutes. Remove the lid. The eggs should be

Method
Roasting

Completion Time
About 30 minutes total time

Dutch Oven Placement
10-inch Dutch oven
Approximately 6 coals on top and 10 coals on bottom

10-inch skillet
14 coals on the bottom

TOP PLACEMENT

BOTTOM PLACEMENT

mostly set by this time. Tip the Dutch oven to a 45-degree angle and then slide your spatula under one half of the omelet and fold it over. Remove the Dutch oven from the heat and let it sit for 5 minutes. Remove omelets and serve.

Biscuits and Gravy
THE BISCUITS

Method
Baking

Completion Time
1 hour

Dutch Oven Placement
12-inch Dutch oven
Approximately 14 coals on
top and 10 on the bottom

THIS IS ONE OF MY FAMILY'S favorite meals. It's rich and will stick to your ribs all day, and for a camping or hunting trip, it's hard to beat this Southern classic. This recipe came from my wife's family. We enjoy these biscuits anytime, whether slathered in butter and honey or covered in the sawmill gravy (recipe follows).

2 cups flour	2 tsp. sugar
4 tsp. baking powder	½ cup shortening
½ tsp. cream of tartar	⅔ cup milk
½ tsp. salt	

 Sift the dry ingredients together. Cut in the shortening until it is in pea-sized clumps. Stir in the milk and roll dough out into a 1-inch-thick sheet. Cut out the biscuits to the desired size and place in a well-greased and warm 12-inch Dutch oven and bake until the tops are golden. Turn them out of the Dutch oven and let them cool for 5 minutes before eating. Caution: leaving the biscuits in the Dutch oven can cause them to overcook.

AT HOME: Place your Dutch oven in a 350-degree oven. Leave the lid off and bake until the sides and tops are gold in color.

TOP PLACEMENT

BOTTOM PLACEMENT

Method
Stewing

Completion Time
About 30 minutes

Dutch Oven Placement
10-inch Dutch oven
Approximately 14 coals
on bottom

10- or 12-inch skillet
Approximately 14 coals
on bottom

TOP PLACEMENT

BOTTOM PLACEMENT

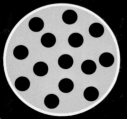

Biscuits and Gravy
THE SAWMILL GRAVY

THIS IS A TIME-HONORED Southern staple. I tried out lots of other recipes until I finally settled on this one as my favorite. The flavor from the roux and sausage combined with the silkiness of the cream makes it a standout. I wouldn't recommend this if you're on a diet, but if you want to taste comfort food at its best, this is it.

1 lb. ground breakfast sausage (I prefer maple flavored)

¼ cup canola oil

¼ stick butter (do not use margarine)

⅓ cup flour

3 cups milk

Black pepper to taste

1 cup heavy cream

In a skillet, begin to brown the sausage after chopping it to the desired size and texture. In the Dutch oven, pour in the oil and add the butter. Stir until the butter is melted. Add in the flour a little at a time, whisking it in and making sure it does not clump. When all the flour is in, stir the roux until it turns dark blond. Add the milk. Drain the fat from the sausage and add it to the roux and milk mixture. Add the black pepper. Cover and stew the sauce for 10 minutes. The sauce should be fairly thick; if it is not, then mix 2 tablespoons of flour with some water. Dump the flour and water into the sauce and stir it well. Do this until the mixture is the desired thickness. Remove the Dutch oven from the coals. Slowly drizzle the

cream on top of the sauce, but do not mix. Cover the sauce and let it sit for 5 minutes. Slowly stir and fold the cream in. Serve over the top of your warm biscuits.

 AT HOME: Use your Dutch oven and skillet on your range top set to medium heat.

Method
Stewing

Completion Time
Less than 1 hour

Dutch Oven Placement
12-inch Dutch oven
Approximately 14 coals
on bottom

TOP PLACEMENT

BOTTOM PLACEMENT

CRÊPES

MY FAMILY LOVES CRÊPES for breakfast. We fill them with all sorts of fruit and fresh whipped cream. The dome of the Dutch oven lid makes it perfect for forming crêpes. You can remove the vanilla and sugar to make dinner crêpes. These are great filled with chicken, sour cream, and lettuce.

1½ cups flour	3 Tbsp. melted butter
2 eggs	½ tsp. vanilla
¾ cup milk	3 Tbsp. sugar
½ tsp. salt	

 Mix all the ingredients together. Place the lid of a 12-inch Dutch oven upside down on a trivet. Place a checkerboard of coals underneath the lid. Grease the lid well. Pour the crêpe batter into the center of the lid and, using a pastry knife, spread the batter up on the sides of the lid, making it thin. When the top loses its gloss, the crêpe is done. Do not flip the crêpe to cook the other side. Remove it and stack it into the Dutch oven itself with 3 coals underneath it to keep the crêpes warm. Stack the crêpes top to bottom or they will stick together. When you serve the crêpes, place the fruit and cream on the top side and roll them up.

AT HOME: Use a skillet on your range top turned to medium heat.

Crêpes

Method
Baking

Completion Time
5 hours to overnight

Dutch Oven Placement
**12-inch Dutch oven
Approximately 16 coals on top
and 10 coals on bottom**

TOP PLACEMENT

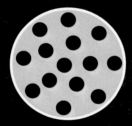

BOTTOM PLACEMENT

Matt's CINNAMON ROLLS

CINNAMON ROLLS, when done right, are some of the best things in the world to eat for breakfast. Nothing will stir taste buds more than the smell of freshly baked Dutch oven cinnamon rolls. These take a little time; plan ahead or make them the night before and chill the dough.

FOR THE DOUGH:

Use the Basic White Bread recipe on page 50.

FOR THE FILLING:

1 stick butter, melted

White sugar to cover

Cinnamon to taste; use enough to cover

Raisins to taste (optional)

Orange zest to cover lightly (optional)

FOR THE FROSTING:

Use the Cream Cheese Frosting recipe found on page 146.

IF YOU WANT ORANGE ROLLS:

Add 1 teaspoon of orange zest and 4 tablespoons of orange juice concentrate to the frosting.

 Knead the dough until it is smooth, elastic, and easy to handle. Chill dough for a few minutes. Stretch and roll the dough out into a rectangle. Brush the dough with the melted butter. Sprinkle on the sugar and cinnamon as well as the optional raisins and orange zest. Roll up the dough and wrap it in greased parchment paper. Let it sit in the fridge or cooler until it's completely chilled. It works well to do this the night before. When the dough is chilled, using a sharp, straight knife or some dental floss, cut the rolled dough into 1-inch-thick slices. Set them in a well-greased and warm 12-inch Dutch oven so the sides touch slightly. Let them rise for 30 minutes. Spray the tops with water and bake them for 30–40 minutes or until the tops are golden. Remove the Dutch oven from the heat. Let the rolls cool for 10 minutes; then pour the frosting on them and spread it around with a basting brush. Enjoy the sticky fun.

AT HOME: Place the Dutch oven in a 350-degree oven. Leave the lid off. The rolls are done when the tops are barely brown.

Chapter EIGHT

BREADS

MORE THAN ANYTHING ELSE in this book, breadmaking is an art form, and it takes a lot of practice to learn how to do right. My Grandma was famous for making breads, and she made loaves almost daily. I loved going to her house and watching her make bread. I can say now that I enjoy it as much as she did. Not just the eating of fresh bread part, either (I think everyone enjoys that part). I enjoy watching the yeast work, feeling the dough in my hands, and creating something beautiful. In this chapter, I will explain what has taken me years to learn. These tips and techniques will help you to make nice breads. To truly become proficient, you need to cook, cook, and cook some more. The more often you practice, the better your breads will become.

Method
Baking

Completion Time
3 hours

Dutch Oven Placement
For rolls: 12-inch Dutch oven
Approximately 14 coals on top
and 10 coals on bottom

For loaf: 10-inch Dutch oven
Approximately 12 coals on top
and 8 coals on bottom

**TOP
PLACEMENT**

**BOTTOM
PLACEMENT**

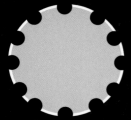

Basic
WHITE BREAD

THIS RECIPE IS THE BASIS of many recipes throughout this book. Though it is used often for other recipes, it makes fantastic rolls or bread just how it is. If you learn and perfect this recipe, you will be well on your way to cooking all sorts of great baked items.

2 tsp. SAF or dry yeast	2 tsp. salt
½ cup sugar	¼ cup warm milk
1½ cups warm water	3–5 cups white flour to stiffen
1½ cups white flour	1 whipped egg (optional)

Begin by dissolving the yeast and the sugar in the warm water. Let the mixture sit for 10 minutes or until you see bubbles or blooms of yeast on the top. Stir in the 1½ cups flour and let it sit for 30–45 minutes. This is an important step in developing the gluten. Stir in the salt and milk. Stir in the 3–5 cups of flour a little at a time until the dough becomes too thick to stir. Turn the dough out onto a well-floured board and sift flour on top of your dough. Knead the dough by folding it and rolling it, adding flour as needed throughout the process. Add the flour a little at a time until the dough is just barely workable but a little sticky. Knead the dough until it becomes quite elastic and springy.

If you want rolls, tear off golf ball–sized dough balls and roll them in your hands. Place them down in a well-greased, warm Dutch oven. Let the dough balls rise for 20 minutes. Cover the Dutch oven and bake for 20–30 minutes or until the tops are golden. If you want a shiny top, brush the tops with a whipped

egg before you let the rolls rise and again after 10 minutes of cooking. Check the rolls every 10 minutes and rotate the Dutch oven and lid if needed—if you see a hot spot. Feel free to move the coals around the lid if you see some rolls getting brown faster than others.

If you want to do bread, form a round ball by turning the bottom edge of the dough in on itself several times and pinching the seams together. Set it seam-side down in a 10-inch Dutch oven. Let it rise for 20 minutes and then cut a seam at the top and bake for 30–40 minutes.

 AT HOME: Place the Dutch in a 375-degree oven. Do not use a lid. The bread is done when the top and sides are golden.

Method
Baking

Completion Time
3 hours

Dutch Oven Placement

FOR ROLLS: 12-inch Dutch oven
**Approximately 16 coals on top
and 10 coals on bottom**

FOR LOAF: 10-inch Dutch oven
**Approximately 12 coals on top
and 8 coals on bottom**

TOP
PLACEMENT

BOTTOM
PLACEMENT

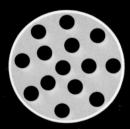

Honey Whole
WHEAT ROLLS

THIS IS A GREAT WHOLE WHEAT RECIPE. The whole wheat is complimented by the honey and is full of flavor. This recipe is not dry and crumbly like a lot of whole wheat breads. Kneading it takes some work, but the rewards are worth it. You can make these into a loaf or rolls; either one works great.

2 tsp. yeast

1/3 cup honey

1½ cups warm water

1¼ cups whole wheat flour

2 tsp. salt

¼ cup milk

1 cup whole wheat flour

2–3 cups white flour to stiffen and dust

1 whipped egg (optional)

Begin by dissolving the yeast and the honey in the warm water. Let it sit for 10 minutes or until you see bubbles or blooms of yeast on the top. Stir in the 1¼ cups whole wheat flour and let the mixture sit for 30–45 minutes. This is an important step in developing the gluten. Stir in the salt and milk. Stir in the 1 cup whole wheat flour a little at a time until it becomes too thick to stir. Turn the dough out onto a well-floured board and sift the white flour on top of your dough. Knead the dough by folding it and rolling it, adding flour as needed throughout the process. Add the flour a little at a time until the dough is barely workable but a little sticky. Knead the dough until it becomes quite elastic and springy. Tear off golf ball–sized dough balls and roll them in your hands. Place the dough balls in a well-greased, warm Dutch oven. Let them rise for 20 minutes. Cover the Dutch oven and bake for 20–30 minutes or until the tops are golden. If you want a shiny

MATT PELTON

top, brush the tops with a whipped egg before you let the rolls rise and again after 10 minutes of cooking. Check the rolls every 10 minutes and rotate the Dutch oven and lid if needed—if you see a hot spot. Feel free to move the coals around the lid if you see some rolls getting brown faster than others.

If you want to do bread, form a round ball by turning the bottom in on itself. Set it seam-side down in a 10-inch Dutch oven. Let the dough rise for 20 minutes and then cut a seam at the top and bake for 30–40 minutes.

 AT HOME: Place the Dutch in a 375-degree oven. Do not use the lid.

Method
Baking

Completion Time
Overnight or 3 hours

Dutch Oven Placement
14-inch Dutch oven for steaming
Approximately 18 coals on top
and bottom

12-inch Dutch oven for loaf
Approximately 12 coals on top
and 8 coals on bottom

**TOP
PLACEMENT**

**BOTTOM
PLACEMENT**

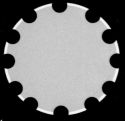

Rustic
TUSCAN BREAD

THIS IS THE BREAD RECIPE we used to win the 2012 IDOS World Championship Cook-Off. It's an artisan bread in that it uses a biga starter. To get the chewy and crispy crust typical of an artisan bread, you need to cook it on a pizza stone placed on a trivet in a 14-inch Dutch oven filled with water. You can cook a fantastic bread in the 10-inch Dutch oven, but the crust will be soft. The flavors of the fermented wheat are amazing, and you will fall in love with this bread.

FOR THE BIGA STARTER:

1 tsp. yeast

¼ cup sugar

¾ cup warm water

¾ cup whole wheat flour

1 tsp. salt

1–2 cups white flour to stiffen

FOR THE DOUGH:

2 tsp. yeast

⅓ cup sugar

1½ cups warm water

1¼ cup wheat flour

2 tsp. salt

The biga starter

2–3 cups white flour to stiffen and dust

Start the biga at least 24 hours before you make the bread. To make the biga, dissolve the yeast and sugar in the warm water. Wait 10 minutes or until you can see bubbles or blooms of yeast on top of the liquid. Stir in the wheat flour and let it rest for 30 minutes. Stir in the salt. Add the white

flour a little at a time until it is too hard to stir. Turn the dough out onto a well-floured board and knead the flour into the dough until it becomes manageable and smooth. Place the dough in a well-oiled plastic bag or airtight container. Let the biga sit 24–48 hours at room temperature; if it will be sitting for longer than that, put it in the fridge. Start the dough in the same way as the biga and add the biga at the same time you add the salt. Add the white flour and turn it out on a floured board. Knead the dough well until it is elastic. Tear off a chunk of the dough equal to 1 cup and set aside for the next biga. If you are steaming the bread, form the bread and place it in a floured proofing basket seam-side up. If you are just cooking the bread normally, set it in a slightly warmed and greased 10-inch Dutch oven. Let the dough rise for 40 minutes. Slash the top of the bread to allow for expansion. If you are steaming the bread, turn the bread onto a heated pizza stone. Have your 14-inch Dutch oven preheated as hot as you can get it. Place the trivet in the bottom of the Dutch oven. Pour 5 cups water in the bottom of the pan. Set the loaf and the pizza stone into the Dutch. With water, spray the bread and oven well. Bake for 45 minutes or until the bread is brown and glossy on the top. If you are cooking a loaf in a 10-inch Dutch oven, spray it with water after it has proofed and bake for 30–40 minutes or until brown on top.

 AT HOME: Place the Dutch oven in a 375-degree oven. The bread is done when the tops and sides start to brown.

Method
Baking

Completion Time
**Overnight with the starter,
4 hours prep and cook time**

Dutch Oven Placement
**14-inch Dutch oven
Approximately 20 coals on
top and 16 on bottom**

10-inch pizza stone on a trivet

TOP PLACEMENT

BOTTOM PLACEMENT

Country FRENCH BREAD

THIS IS A VERY OLD RECIPE. It has been adapted over the years and made into baguettes, rolls, and, more recently, an Artisan bread. The original bread was cooked on a stone hearth. The recipe here will replicate the original style of the bread. You can use the bread for cooking baguettes if you want. To continue this bread remove about 1 cup of the dough after the dough is kneaded and set it aside in a crock container. If you don't plan on cooking bread for another week or longer, the starter must be kept in the fridge.

FOR THE STARTER:

¾ cup water

2 Tbsp. sugar

1 tsp. yeast

½ tsp. salt

Approximately 2 cups flour to stiffen and knead

FOR THE DOUGH:

1 tsp. yeast

⅓ cup sugar

1¼ cups warm water

¼ cup wheat flour

1 cup white flour

The starter from the day before, approximately 1 cup

1 tsp. salt

Approximately 4 cups white flour to stiffen and dust

 The night before, mix the ingredients together for the starter. Knead the dough until it is elastic and smooth

Place in a bowl and cover in plastic wrap. When you are ready to make the bread, dissolve the yeast in a bowl with the sugar and the water. Let it sit for about 15 minutes. The yeast should be bubbling or developing blooms on the top. Stir in the wheat flour and the 1 cup of white flour. Add the starter and mix it in well. Add the salt and add the white flour a little at a time until the dough begins to be stiff. Turn the dough out on a board and knead for several minutes until it is elastic and smooth. Add flour as needed until the dough is no longer sticky. Remove about 1 cup of the dough and set it aside for the next loaf of bread. Form a ball with the dough by pinching the dough and turning the edges inward in on itself. Set the dough in a bowl (wood bowls are best for flavor). Cover it and set aside for at least an hour and no more than three hours. Remove the dough carefully from the bowl and set inside a proofing basket to rise. Let the bread rise for an hour or until the dough is nearly to the top of the 10-inch proofing basket. Preheat the Dutch oven for 15 minutes prior to cooking. Turn the dough out onto the pizza stone and place the stone inside of the Dutch oven, on a trivet. Pour about a cup of water into the bottom of the Dutch oven using a funnel, taking care to not pour any on the bread. Bake for about 40 minutes or until the crust is golden and if you tap the bread it sounds hollow. Let the bread relax for a few minutes before slicing.

AT HOME: Follow the directions above. Bake in a pre-heated oven set to 425 degrees. Bake with the lid on the Dutch oven.

Method
Baking

Completion Time
4 hours

Dutch Oven Placement
10-inch Dutch oven
Approximately 12 coals on
top and 8 on the bottom

10-inch skillet
14 coals on bottom

TOP PLACEMENT

BOTTOM PLACEMENT

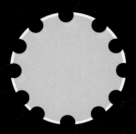

Apple Cinnamon BREAD

THIS IS A VERY SIMPLE but very good treat. It is best if cooked as a loaf and not rolls. You can mix the filling in at random or roll it for a pretty presentation.

FOR THE DOUGH:

Use the Basic White Bread recipe on page 50.

FOR THE FILLING:

½ stick butter

1 green apple cut into small chunks

2 tsp. cinnamon

½ tsp. nutmeg

¼ cup brown sugar

Follow the Basic White Bread recipe directions to begin. In a 10-inch skillet, melt the butter and sauté the apple chunks until they are tender. Remove from the heat and mix in the cinnamon and nutmeg. Let mixture cool to room temperature. When you add the salt and milk into the basic dough mixture, before kneading, add the apples, spices, and brown sugar. Add the flour and knead the bread following the Basic White Bread recipe. Form your loaf and place in a well-oiled, warm 10-inch Dutch oven. Let the loaf rise for 45 minutes. Brush the top with optional egg and bake for 30–45 minutes or until the top is golden.

 AT HOME: Place the Dutch oven in a 350-degree oven. The bread is done when the top and sides are golden. The internal temperature should read 200 degrees.

MATT PELTON

Parmesan-Crusted
ROLLS

THESE ROLLS ARE NICE and savory, and they go well with a lot of meals. Feel free to experiment by adding herbs into the dough. I find that using freshly grated Parmesan may cost a little more, but the price is worth the flavor.

FOR THE DOUGH:

Use the Basic White Bread recipe on page 50.

FOR THE HERBS AND TOPPING:

½ tsp. dill

1 tsp. fresh parsley

½ tsp. thyme

1 tsp. dry onions

1 egg for egg wash

¼ cup freshly grated Parmesan cheese

 Follow the Basic White Bread directions to begin, but when you stir in the salt and milk, also stir in the dill, parsley, thyme, and dry onions. Knead the dough until it is elastic. Form rolls to your desired size and place into a well-greased, 12-inch Dutch oven. Let rolls rise for 20 minutes. Bake them for 10 minutes and then open the oven and brush the tops of the rolls with the egg wash. To create an egg wash, whip 1 egg in a small bowl; brush the wash onto the dough using a basting brush. Bake for another 10 minutes; then open and cover the rolls with the Parmesan cheese. Bake for 10 minutes more or until the cheese is melted and the tops are browned.

AT HOME: Place the Dutch in a 350-degree oven. Do not use the lid. The rolls are done when the tops are browned.

Method
Baking

Completion Time
3 hours

Dutch Oven Placement
12-inch Dutch oven
Approximately 14 coals on top and 10 on the bottom

TOP
PLACEMENT

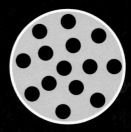

BOTTOM
PLACEMENT

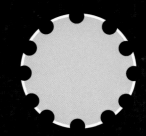

Regional Sourdough Bread

Regional Sourdough BREAD

Method
Baking

Completion Time
7 days or 6 hours

Dutch Oven Placement
10-inch Dutch oven
Approximately 12 coals on
top and 8 coals on bottom

GIVING YOU A SAN FRANCISCO sourdough recipe is impossible because you would have to live there to be able to create the flavor. Every region has its own strain of yeast, and every yeast strain tastes a little different. The effect is the same—a great-tasting bread.

FOR THE STARTER:

2 cups water

2 Tbsp. pineapple juice

2 cups flour

FOR THE DOUGH:

1½ cups warm water

1 cup flour

¼ cup sugar

Starter

2 tsp. salt

2–3 cups flour, for stiffening and dusting

A week before you want to cook the bread, mix the starter ingredients and set aside at room temperature. After one week, remove the crusty layer of dough; what is left is your starter. It should be bubbly and smell sour. For the dough, mix the water, 1 cup flour, starter, and sugar together. Let it sit for 4 hours or overnight if you want. Remove 1½ cups of the mix: this will be your starter for the next time you cook the bread. The starter can stay in the fridge for several weeks but must be fed and used or it will die and rot. The longer you use a starter the better it will taste as you develop your regional taste. Add the salt and stir in the 2–3 cups flour

TOP PLACEMENT

BOTTOM PLACEMENT

a little at a time until it forms a dough. Knead it until it is smooth but sticky. Place it in a warm and well-greased 10-inch Dutch oven. Let the dough rise for 3–4 hours. Carefully close the lid and bake the dough for 30–40 minutes or until it is browned on top.

(Hint: I usually let the dough rise in the same spot as I plan to cook it. Moving the Dutch oven around can cause the dough to fall, leaving it dense.)

 AT HOME: Place the Dutch on a 375-degree oven. Do not use the lid. The rolls are done when the top is browned.

German Rye BREAD

Method
Baking

Completion Time
Overnight or 4 hours

Dutch Oven Placement
10-inch Dutch oven
Approximately 12 coals on
top and 8 coals on bottom

THE GERMAN RYE BREAD differs a lot from a Jewish rye bread. Jewish rye has caraway seed, and the rye is strong and pronounced. The German rye is sweeter and has a more delicate texture. It uses a biga starter, so you will have to plan ahead to make it. It will be worth it though.

FOR THE BIGA STARTER:

1 cup warm water

1 tsp. yeast

¼ cup molasses

¼ cup sugar

½ cup rye flour

¼ cup whole wheat flour

FOR THE DOUGH:

1½ cups warm water

⅓ cup white sugar

2 tsp. yeast

1 cup rye flour

¼ cup whole wheat flour

¼ cup molasses

2 tsp. salt

1 Tbsp. cocoa

3–4 cups white flour, to stiffen and dust

TOP PLACEMENT

BOTTOM PLACEMENT

 Mix the ingredients for the biga starter the night before; cover it and let it sit. The next day for the dough, mix the water, sugar, and yeast. Let the mixture sit for 10 minutes or until the yeast is bubbly. Add the rye and wheat flours; mix well and let sit for 30 minutes. Add the starter, molasses, salt, and cocoa. Add the white flour a little at a time until it is too stiff to stir. Dump the dough out on a well-floured

board. Knead the dough until it is workable and smooth. The longer you knead it, the better the end product will be. Form a loaf and set the bread in a well-greased, 10-inch Dutch oven with the seam side down. I like to spread a little cornmeal on the bottom of the Dutch oven first. Let it rise for 1 hour. Slash the top and cook it for about an hour or until the loaf is brown on the top.

 AT HOME: Place the Dutch in a 375-degree oven without the lid. Bake until browned.

Southern-Style CORNBREAD

I LOVE A GOOD CORNBREAD, and Dutch ovens are the best way to cook a good cornbread. This is a Southern-style cornbread because it has corn and bacon mixed in. In the South, they cook it in a skillet on a stovetop. I prefer it in a Dutch oven because the texture is more cake-like and fluffy.

1 cup white cornmeal

2 cups buttermilk

1¾ cups white flour

1½ tsp. baking powder

1 tsp. baking soda

½ tsp. cream of tartar

1 tsp. salt

⅓ cup white sugar

⅓ cup brown sugar

3 large eggs

2 Tbsp. honey

½ stick butter, melted

2 cups fresh or frozen corn kernels (do not use canned corn)

½ lb. cooked bacon, chopped (optional)

2 Tbsp. bacon grease or vegetable oil to grease the Dutch oven

 Mix all the ingredients together and pour into a warm Dutch oven greased with the bacon grease. (For an extra fluffy cornbread, soak the cornmeal in the buttermilk the night before and then mix everything else together.) Bake for 40–50 minutes or until you can insert a knife in the center and have it come out clean.

AT HOME: Place the Dutch in a 350-degree oven. Do not use the lid.

Method
Baking

Completion Time
1½ hours

Dutch Oven Placement
10-inch Dutch oven
Approximately 12 coals on
top and 8 coals on bottom

TOP PLACEMENT

BOTTOM PLACEMENT

Southwestern-Style Cornbread

Southwestern-Style CORNBREAD

I LOVE A GOOD CORNBREAD, and Dutch ovens are the best way to cook a good cornbread. This is the same recipe as the Yankee-Style Cornbread (68). The difference is the added corn and roasted jalapeños.

1 Tbsp. oil

¾ cup chopped and roasted jalapeño peppers

1½ cups yellow cornmeal

2½ cups milk

1½ cups white flour

1½ tsp. baking powder

1½ tsp. baking soda

½ tsp. cream of tartar

2 tsp. salt

½ cup white sugar

½ cup brown sugar

3 large eggs

1 stick butter, melted

1 cup frozen corn kernels

 In a 10-inch Dutch oven, heat up some oil. Slice the jalapeños in half and remove the veins and seeds. Roast the jalapeños for 15–20 minutes or until they are starting to brown. Remove from the pan and dice them into small pieces. Mix all the ingredients together and pour into a warm Dutch oven, greased well. Bake for 40–50 minutes or until you can insert a knife in the center and have it come out clean.

AT HOME: Place the Dutch in a 350-degree oven. Do not use the lid.

Method
Baking

Completion Time
1½ hours

Dutch Oven Placement
10-inch Dutch oven
Approximately 12 coals on top and 8 coals on bottom

TOP PLACEMENT

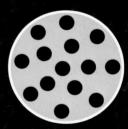

BOTTOM PLACEMENT

Method
Baking

Completion Time
1½ hours

Dutch Oven Placement
10-inch Dutch oven
Approximately 12 coals on
top and 8 on the bottom

TOP PLACEMENT

BOTTOM PLACEMENT

Yankee-Style CORNBREAD

I LOVE A GOOD CORNBREAD, and Dutch ovens are the best way to cook a good cornbread. This recipe uses yellow cornmeal and is sweeter than its Southern cousin.

1½ cups yellow cornmeal	2 tsp. salt
2½ cups milk	½ cup white sugar
1½ cups white flour	½ cup brown sugar
1½ tsp. baking powder	3 large eggs
1½ tsp. baking soda	1 stick butter, melted
½ tsp. cream of tartar	

 Mix all the ingredients together and pour into a warm Dutch oven, greased well. Bake for 40–50 minutes or until you can insert a knife in the center and have it come out clean.

 AT HOME: Place the Dutch in a 350-degree oven. Do not use the lid.

Chapter NINE

SOUPS, STEWS, AND CHILIS

I LOVE TO COOK SOUPS in a Dutch oven. We have soup perhaps once a week in my home. They are nutritious and taste great, especially with some freshly made rolls. Hard to beat that kind of comfort food. A rule for making a great soup: make sure that you're able to get the full flavor out of every ingredient. Follow the process and don't get in a hurry, and you will have exceptional dishes.

Method
Stewing

Completion Time
1–2 hours

Dutch Oven Placement
12-inch Dutch oven
Approximately 16 coals
on bottom

TOP
PLACEMENT

BOTTOM
PLACEMENT

French Chicken
SOUP

THIS IS MY FAVORITE of all the soups I make. It has a silky texture and an amazing flavor. Make sure that you use the Spanish saffron to get the right flavor. It's an expensive spice, but you don't need much for the soup.

½ stick butter

4 Tbsp. olive oil

1 cup finely chopped onions

½ cup finely cut celery with greens

½ cup finely chopped carrots

1–2 lbs. chopped chicken thighs

1 pinch Spanish saffron (do not use Mexican saffron—it's not the same thing)

2 (14-oz.) cans chicken stock or broth (stock is better)

4 oz. shredded cheddar cheese

½ pint heavy cream

 In your Dutch oven, melt butter in the olive oil. Slowly stir in the onions, celery, and carrots. Cover and cook the mixture for 20 minutes, stirring as needed. Add the chicken and saffron; let the soup simmer for 15 minutes until the yellow liquid is covering the chicken. Add the chicken stock and simmer until the liquid is cloudy and golden in color. Heat it up to high and slowly stir in the cheese a little at a time until it is fully dissolved. Remove Dutch oven from the heat. Shake or lightly whip the cream. Slowly pour the cream on top of the soup. Do not stir. Let it sit for 10–15 minutes and then slowly fold the cream into the soup.

AT HOME: Place the Dutch oven on the range top with the heat on medium-low. Increase the heat to high when melting the cheese into the soup.

Split Pea SOUP

MANY PEOPLE DO NOT ENJOY split pea soup. I believe this is because they have not tried one made well. I love this soup despite its color. It has fantastic flavor and a lot of richness. It reminds me of being a kid, coming home in the winter, and having a large bowl of warm soup.

½ stick butter	1 lb. cubed ham
1 cup finely chopped onion	3 (14-oz.) cans chicken broth
½ cup finely chopped celery	2 bay leaves
½ cup finely chopped carrots	1 lb. dried split peas

 Begin by melting the butter in the bottom of your Dutch oven. Add the onions, celery, and carrots. Cover and simmer for 20 minutes, stirring occasionally. Add the ham, 2 cans chicken broth, and bay leaves. Simmer for 30 minutes. Add the third can of chicken broth and the split peas. Simmer for another hour. Add water as needed and scrape the bottom of the Dutch oven to keep the peas from burning. The soup is done when the peas are dissolved.

AT HOME: Set the Dutch oven on the range top set to medium-low heat.

Method
Stewing

Completion Time
3 hours

Dutch Oven Placement
12-inch Dutch oven
Approximately 16 coals on bottom, refresh every hour

TOP PLACEMENT

BOTTOM PLACEMENT

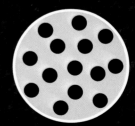

Ham and Bean Soup

Ham and Bean SOUP

THIS SOUP REMINDS ME of easier times, hanging out in a hunting lodge with a pot full of this soup sitting on the wood-burning stove. We would continually add to the pot every day. It was nice to be able to come in from the cold and serve up a bowl full of hot soup.

1 onion, finely chopped

1 Tbsp. oil

1 lb. diced ham

3 (14-oz.) cans great northern beans

3 bay leaves

2 (14-oz.) cans chicken broth

 Begin by sautéing the onions in a little oil in the Dutch oven until they burn. The onions should be black in spots to get the flavor for what you need. Add the remaining ingredients to the Dutch oven. Be sure to rinse the beans well beforehand (rinsed canned beans will cut down on gas production when you eat them). Simmer for 30 minutes. When the soup is done, the liquid will look milky. If you want a thicker soup, mash the beans with a potato masher while cooking.

AT HOME: Set the Dutch oven on the range top set to medium-low heat.

Method
Stewing

Completion Time
1 hour

Dutch Oven Placement
12-inch Dutch oven
Approximately 16 coals on the bottom

TOP PLACEMENT

BOTTOM PLACEMENT

Method
Stewing

Completion Time
1½ hours

Dutch Oven Placement
12-inch Dutch oven
Approximately 16 coals
on bottom

TOP PLACEMENT

BOTTOM PLACEMENT

Pork and New Potato STEW

THIS RECIPE WAS CONCEIVED from a case of what-you-got stew. We were on an elk hunt in southern Utah and this happened to be what-we-got. We liked it so well that now cooking it up is a hunting tradition. This stew is simple to make and tastes great.

1 onion, chopped fine

½ stick butter

2 lbs. pork, cubed (any type)

Flour, to thicken to desired amount

1 (14-oz.) can chicken broth

2 (14-oz.) cans new potatoes or 3 cups fresh new potatoes

 In the Dutch oven, begin by browning the onion in the butter. Add the pork and stir until it is browned. Add a bit of the flour and stir it in, coating the meat. Add the broth and the new potatoes. Simmer for 30–45 minutes or until the pork is tender. Add water or flour to get the consistency you want.

AT HOME: Set the Dutch oven on the range top set to medium-low heat.

Caldo de Res
(SOUP OF BEEF)

T HIS MEXICAN SOUP is more of a meal in liquid than it is a soup. Serve this soup with tortillas, limes, and pickled jalapeños.

1 (2- to 3-lb.) beef chuck or picnic roast

1 onion, quartered

4 baby zucchinis, quartered

3 ears corn, cut into 3-inch pieces

1 head cabbage, cut into chunks

1 (14-oz.) can diced tomatoes

½ cup sugar

3 bay leaves

1 (4-oz.) can pickled jalapeño slices

3 (14-oz.) cans chicken broth

1 tsp. cumin

1 tsp. oregano

1 lime, zested and squeezed

2 tsp. powdered New Mexico chilies

 Add all the ingredients into the Dutch Oven (that you can fit around the beef) and stew for 3–5 hours, adding more broth as needed. To serve, pull off a chunk of beef, corn, zucchini, and cabbage. Add a little broth and eat in tortillas.

AT HOME: Set the Dutch oven on the range top set to medium-low heat.

Method
Stewing

Completion Time
1½ hours

Dutch Oven Placement
**12-inch Dutch oven
Approximately 16 coals on the bottom**

TOP PLACEMENT

BOTTOM PLACEMENT

Hunters STEW

Method
Stewing

Completion Time
1½ hours

Dutch Oven Placement
12-inch Dutch oven
Approximately 16 coals
on bottom

TOP PLACEMENT

BOTTOM PLACEMENT

THIS IS MY TAKE ON A GERMAN Wiener schnitzel. It's very similar to a Salisbury steak recipe with the potatoes cooked in the stew as well. Use any type of red meat you would like. I call it Hunters Stew because we would use meat from whatever we were hunting to make it.

2–3 lbs. thin-cut steaks (tougher steaks like shoulder or flank work best)	1 large onion, left whole
	4 garlic cloves, peeled and left whole
Flour to dust steaks	¼ cup Worcestershire sauce
2 Tbsp. butter	2 cups brown mushrooms, chopped (Italian or portobello)
¼ cup oil	
¼ cup flour	2 (14-oz.) cans new potatoes
3 (14-oz.) cans beef broth	Salt and pepper to taste

 To begin, pound the steaks with a meat mallet or the back end of a heavy knife (this process is cleaner when you put meat between two sheets of plastic). Dust the steaks with flour. In the bottom of a 12-inch Dutch oven, heat up some butter. Sear the steaks well on both sides so they are browned. Remove the steaks and let them rest. Add the oil to the Dutch oven and scrape the bottom well. Slowly stir in the flour and whisk it until it is blond in color. Slowly add 2 cans beef broth and stir it well. Add the onion, garlic, and Worcestershire sauce. Stew for 15 minutes. Add the mushrooms, steaks, and potatoes. Cover and stew for 20–30 minutes. Add the third can of beef broth if the liquid level gets too low.

AT HOME: Set the Dutch oven on a range top set to medium-low heat.

New England Clam CHOWDER

MOST PEOPLE ARE FAMILIAR with this classic clam chowder—the thick creamy chowder that warms you up on a cold day. I love it anytime.

¼ cup canola oil

½ stick butter

1 onion, finely chopped

1 cup sliced celery

⅓ cup flour

8 cups milk

2 small cans baby clams cut into strips

2 (14-oz.) cans new potatoes cut into bite-sized chunks

½ tsp. celery seed

Black pepper to taste

½ pint heavy cream

 Heat up the oil and butter in the bottom of a Dutch oven. Add the onions and celery. Stew until the onions are clear. Slowly stir in the flour—stir it well until it is coated completely. Slowly add the milk, also stirring it well. Add the baby clams, potatoes, celery seed, and pepper. Stew for 1 hour. If the chowder is not thick enough, stir in one-to-one ratio of flour and water, mixed well, a little at a time until the chowder is fairly thick. Remove the Dutch oven from the heat and let it sit for 5 minutes. Shake the cream well so it is frothy and slowly pour over the top of the chowder. Let the cream sit for 5 minutes; then fold it into the chowder.

AT HOME: Set the Dutch oven on the range top set to medium-low heat.

Method
Stewing

Completion Time
1½ hours

Dutch Oven Placement
12-inch Dutch oven
Approximately 16 coals on the bottom

TOP PLACEMENT

BOTTOM PLACEMENT

Method
Stewing & Roasting

Completion Time
1½ hours

Dutch Oven Placement
12-inch Dutch oven
Approximately 16 coals
on bottom

10-inch Dutch oven
Approximately 14 coals
on bottom, 7 on the top

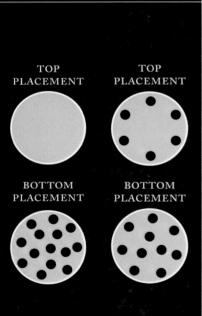

TOP
PLACEMENT

TOP
PLACEMENT

BOTTOM
PLACEMENT

BOTTOM
PLACEMENT

Pork Chile VERDE

THIS IS AN AUTHENTIC chile verde recipe from Mexico. This recipe will feed a number of people as a soup. I like to make a batch and freeze it; then I reheat it later and pour it over enchiladas or over tortilla chips for nachos. Either way you do it, it's good.

5 Anaheim chilies, seeded and veined

2 jalapeños, seeded and veined

1 large onion

½ stick butter

¼ cup oil

⅓ cup white flour

2 (14-oz.) cans chicken broth

5 Roma tomatoes

2–3 lbs. pork, cubed (any type)

2 juiced limes, 1 zested

1 tsp. cumin

2 tsp. oregano

Start by putting the Anaheim chilies, jalapeños, and onion in a 10-inch Dutch oven with a little oil. Roast for about an hour. After the hour, mash them up as good as you can. In the 12-inch Dutch oven, create a roux by melting the butter into the oil and slowly whisking in the flour. Stir often until the roux is dark blond. Slowly add the chicken broth, stirring it in. Add the roasted chili and onions, the tomatoes, and the pork. Add the seasonings. Add the lime juice and zest to the mixture and stew for 1–3 hours or until the tenderness of the pork is what you want. Add liquid (water or more broth) if necessary and thicken with flour if it is too loose.

 AT HOME: Place the chili and onions in the 10-inch Dutch. Place the Dutch in the oven set to 300 degrees for 1 hour with the lid on. Remove the Dutch oven, mash the chili mix, and add to the 12-inch Dutch oven on the range top set to medium-low heat.

Method
Stewing

Completion Time
1½ hours

Dutch Oven Placement
12-inch Dutch oven
Approximately 16 coals
on bottom

TOP PLACEMENT

BOTTOM PLACEMENT

Darn Good CHILI

I HAVE SO MANY CHILI RECIPES that I have a hard time keeping them all straight. In my previous book, *The Cast Iron Chef*, I had several recipes for different kinds of chili. This is the only one I am including in this book because it is far and away my favorite. I love to eat this chili with my Yankee Cornbread recipe from page 68.

1 large onion, chopped fine

2 lbs. cubed beef chuck

1 lb. breakfast sausage links, cut into chunks

3 bay leaves

1 (14-oz.) can crushed tomatoes

1 (14-oz.) can black beans, rinsed and drained

2 (14-oz.) cans pinto beans, rinsed and drained

3 (14-oz.) cans beef broth

2 beef bouillon cubes

3 tsp. chili powder

½ tsp. cumin

¼ cup honey

1 (4-oz.) can diced jalapeños (optional)

3 Tbsp. vinegar

Begin by browning the onions in the bottom of the Dutch oven until they are clear. Stir in the beef and sausage until they are browned. Add the remaining ingredients. Stew for 1 hour. Add liquid if necessary and be sure to scrape the bottom to keep the chili from burning. When the chili is done, you can thicken it by mashing the beans with a potato masher.

AT HOME: Place the Dutch oven on the range top set to medium-low heat.

Chicken TACO SOUP

THIS SOUP IS A FAMILY favorite of ours. We like to crush tortilla chips, add sour cream, and sprinkle some cheese on top.

Method
Stewing

Completion Time
1 hour

Dutch Oven Placement
12-inch Dutch oven
Approximately 16 coals on
the bottom

1 Tbsp. oil

1 small onion, chopped fine

2 lbs. chicken, cubed

1 (14-oz.) can pinto beans, drained and rinsed

1 (14-oz.) can black beans, drained and rinsed

1 (14-oz.) can crushed tomatoes

2 (14-oz.) cans chicken broth

½ cup cooked rice

1 tsp. cumin

1 tsp. New Mexico chili powder

2 bay leaves

4 Tbsp. cider vinegar

1 lime, squeezed

4 Tbsp. brown sugar

1 (4-oz.) can chopped green chilies

½ tsp. oregano

4 corn tortillas, minced

TOP PLACEMENT

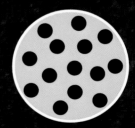

BOTTOM PLACEMENT

In the bottom of your Dutch oven, heat up 1 tablespoon of oil. Add the onions and cook until they are clear and starting to brown (this is important for the flavor). Slowly stir in the chicken. Cover and stew for 15 minutes, stirring occasionally. Add the remaining ingredients except the tortillas. Cover and stew for 45 minutes. Add the tortillas and stir them in. Stew for 5 minutes until the tortillas begin to dissolve.

AT HOME: Place the Dutch oven on range top set to medium-low heat.

Pumpkin
SOUP

Method
Stewing

Completion Time
1 hour

Dutch Oven Placement
12-inch Dutch oven
Approximately 16 coals
on bottom

THIS IS A GREAT FALL-TIME soup. It is very elegant and easy to make. In this recipe, I have listed canned pumpkin in the ingredients, but you can use baked and pureed butternut squash instead for an extra special taste.

1 stick butter

⅓ cup flour

3 (14-oz.) cans vegetable broth

2 cups canned pumpkin

¼ cup brown sugar

½ tsp. nutmeg

1 tsp. salt

1 tsp. cinnamon

½ pint heavy cream

 Begin by melting the butter in the bottom of the Dutch oven. Slowly whisk in the flour and stir it for about 10 minutes; the roux should be blonde in color. Slowly stir in the vegetable broth, pumpkin, brown sugar, and seasonings. Stew for 30 minutes. Remove from the heat and let it sit for 5 minutes. Shake up the cream until it is frothy. Slowly pour the cream into the soup. Let it sit for 5 minutes and then fold the cream into the soup.

 AT HOME: Place the Dutch oven on the range top set to medium-low heat.

**TOP
PLACEMENT**

**BOTTOM
PLACEMENT**

Chapter TEN

MAIN COURSES

MAIN COURSES have always been my strong suit. I think this is because of my love for meat. Even when I was a little kid, I was a carnivore. Every time I cook a piece of meat, I put my heart and soul into it. I've listed some tricks that will help you in each recipe. Follow these tips, because I have spent years trying to find them on my own. As far as the recipes go, have fun and experiment with them.

Method
Baking & Stewing

Completion Time
3½ hours

Dutch Oven Placement
**12-inch Dutch oven
Approximately 14 coals
on top, and 10 coals on bottom**

**10-inch Dutch oven
Approximately 14 coals
on bottom**

TOP
PLACEMENT

TOP
PLACEMENT

BOTTOM
PLACEMENT

BOTTOM
PLACEMENT

Lasagna
ITALIA

THIS IS MY FAVORITE LASAGNA recipe as of late. I learned to make lasagna while living in the north end of Boston forever ago. I fell in love with the rustic flavors of a garden-grown sauce and hand-ground sausage. Though you need not go to those extremes, a handcrafted sauce is easy to do and brings so much more flavor to your lasagna.

1 full head garlic

1 (8-oz.) pkg. lasagna noodles

¼ cup extra virgin olive oil

1½ lbs. sweet Italian sausage (spicy works as well)

1 lb. cremini, Italian brown, or chopped portobello mushrooms

1 lb. grape tomatoes, whole

A few fresh basil leaves

½ lemon, squeezed

3 vine-ripened tomatoes, chopped

8 oz. washed baby spinach leaves

2 lbs. ricotta cheese

2 eggs

2 tsp. sea salt

1 lb. shredded mozzarella cheese

Begin by slowly cutting the very bottom off the head of garlic. Brush it with olive oil and place in the 12-inch Dutch oven for 35 minutes with 6 coals on the bottom and 10 coals on the top. Boil the package of noodles until they are al dente (a little firm). Rinse them well and set aside. Heat up the olive oil in the 10-inch Dutch oven and add the sausage. Stir in the sausage until it is beginning to brown. Add the mushrooms and the whole grape tomatoes. Cover and simmer until the tomatoes burst. Add the basil, lemon juice, and chopped tomatoes. Cover and simmer for 30 minutes, stirring

occasionally. Squeeze most of the roasted garlic into the sauce and cover it with the spinach. Allow the sauce to rest. To build the cheese layer: Dump the ricotta cheese into a bowl. Squeeze the rest of the roasted garlic into the cheese. Whip up the eggs and fold them into the cheese. Add the salt to the cheese. In the 12-inch Dutch oven, add a base layer of noodles, followed by the cheese, and then the sauce/sausage. Cover with the mozzarella cheese. Follow this pattern twice. For the top layer, cover with noodles and the remaining cheese. Bake for 1 hour until the top is browned. The internal temperature should be 180 degrees. Let the lasagna rest for 15 minutes before serving.

 AT HOME: Place the Dutch oven in a 350-degree oven. Bake until the internal temperature reaches 180 degrees.

Roasted Pork Shoulder

Roasted Pork SHOULDER

Method
Roasting

Completion Time
6 hours

Dutch Oven Placement
12-inch Dutch oven
Approximately 10 coals
on top, 14 coals on bottom

THIS WONDERFUL DISH will take you a little time to make, but it is worth the effort. Once you have roasted the pork, you can pull it and serve it and freeze the remaining meat for later treats. This recipe is not so complex on ingredients. It is more the technique in cooking it that makes the difference. It will result in nice bark as well as tender meat that is easy to pull.

1 (5- to 6-lb.) pork shoulder roast (Boston butt)

Tony Chachere's Creole Seasoning (or similar seasoning)

3 cups apple juice

1 cup cider vinegar

¼ cup brown sugar

2 Tbsp. hickory liquid smoke

Your favorite barbecue sauce to taste

Prepare the pork shoulder by removing excess fat on the outside of the meat. Season heavily with the Creole seasoning (you should not be able to see much meat). Wait until the seasoning is wet before cooking. Place a trivet inside the Dutch oven. Set the pork roast on the trivet. Cover and let it roast for 1 hour. In the meantime, mix together the apple juice, vinegar, brown sugar, and liquid smoke. Mix well—this is the mop sauce (you can brush it on with a basting brush or spray it on with a spray bottle). After the first hour, refresh the coals, turn the shoulder over, and brush it with the mop sauce. Continue to follow this process every hour for approximately 5 hours. Take a temperature reading in the center of the meat every half hour. The internal temperature should be between 198 and 205 degrees. When you reach this level,

TOP PLACEMENT

BOTTOM PLACEMENT

it is done. Remove the roast from the heat and let it relax for 15–20 minutes before pulling. Pull the roast and season it lightly with the barbecue sauce of your choice.

 AT HOME: Place the Dutch oven in a 325-degree oven with the lid on.

Rock Salt
RIB ROAST

THIS IS A UNIQUE WAY to cook an amazing holiday roast. The meat itself is a little pricey, but for the couple of times a year you may cook this, it's worth the price.

1 (3- to 4-lb.) bone-in rib-eye roast, at least "choice" grade

¼ cup Dijon mustard

2 tsp. crushed mustard seeds

4 tsp. coarse ground black pepper

½ cup flour

10 lbs. coarse rock salt

 Start by rubbing the roast down with the Dijon mustard (do not put it on the bones). Sprinkle the mustard seed, black pepper, and flour onto the roast. Pat the sprinkled flour into the roast and let it rest at room temperature for 20 minutes. Place a layer of rock salt about an inch thick in the bottom of the Dutch oven. Place the roast bone-side down on top of the rock salt layer. Pour more rock salt all around and pack it in tight to the roast. Roast for 3–4 hours, refreshing coals and checking the temperature every hour. When the center of the roast reaches 130 degrees, pull the roast from the heat and let it relax for 20 minutes. Break the shell off the roast, remove the meat from the bones, and slice into ½-inch slices to serve. This is best served drizzled with a little au jus made from the drippings and some freshly made horseradish sauce.

AT HOME: Place your Dutch oven with the lid on in a 350-degree oven.

Method
Roasting

Completion Time
3–4 hours

Dutch Oven Placement
12-inch deep Dutch oven
Approximately 16 coals on top, 12 coals on bottom

TOP PLACEMENT

BOTTOM PLACEMENT

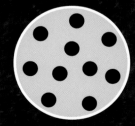

Method
Roasting

Completion Time
3–4 hours

Dutch Oven Placement
**Cast-iron oval roaster or
12-inch Dutch Oven
Approximately 8 coals on top,
and 16 coals on bottom**

TOP PLACEMENT

BOTTOM PLACEMENT

Chuckwagon-Style
BEEF BRISKET

OF ALL THE MEATS OUT THERE, brisket is one of my favorites. There are a number of ways to cook a brisket, but the method that works best is low and slow. When you serve the brisket, slice it across the grain in thin slices: one-eighth to a quarter of an inch. I personally don't care for barbecue sauce on my brisket, but a lot of people like it. For me, nothing is better than just dipping the slices au jus in the bottom of the pan.

1 brisket flat, about 5 lbs.

Tony Chachere's Creole Seasoning to (or similar seasoning)

2 large onions

1 (14-oz.) can beef broth

1 cup apple juice

4 Tbsp. cider vinegar

2 Tbsp. mesquite liquid smoke

Begin by trimming the excess fat from the top of the brisket. You should have about ⅛ inch of fat on the top. Sprinkle the Creole seasoning over the brisket until coated lightly. Cut the onions into thick rings. Mix the beef broth, apple juice, vinegar, and liquid smoke—this is the mop sauce; set it aside in a bowl. When the seasoning on the brisket looks wet, place the onions in the bottom of the Dutch oven and the brisket on top of them. After 1 hour, turn the brisket over, brush the brisket with the mop sauce, and refresh the coals. Follow this process every hour for 3–4 hours. Take a temperature reading in the center of the meat after each hour. The brisket is

done when the internal temperature reads between 198 and 205 degrees. When the brisket is done, remove it from the heat and let it relax for 15–20 minutes before slicing.

 AT HOME: Place the Dutch oven in a 325-degree oven with the lid on.

Method
Roasting

Completion Time
Overnight

Dutch Oven Placement
12-inch deep Dutch oven
Approximately 10 coals
on top, and 16 on bottom

TOP PLACEMENT

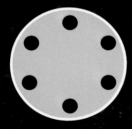

BOTTOM PLACEMENT

Best Dutch Oven
WHOLE CHICKEN

WHOLE CHICKENS CAN be one of the hardest Dutch oven meals to do right. With this recipe and instructions, it will be easy and a definite crowd pleaser.

FOR THE BRINE:

½ gallon cold water

1 cup kosher salt

½ cup brown sugar

1 (12-oz.) can ginger ale

2 tsp. maple flavoring extract

2 Tbsp. black pepper

2 Tbsp. lemon juice or
1 lemon, squeezed

FOR THE BIRD:

1 (2- to 3-lb.) roasting hen

2 large onions, cut into thick rings

2 Tbsp. orange marmalade

¼ cup zesty Italian dressing

Begin by mixing the brine ingredients in a bowl. Score the skin on the chicken with a fork. Place the chicken in the brine and refrigerate overnight (I like to place it in a garbage sack to make sure that it will cover). The next day, remove the chicken from the brine and set it on a wire rack to dry. When the chicken is no longer dripping, cut the onions and place them in the bottom of the Dutch oven. Set the chicken on top and roast for 30 minutes. In a bowl, mix the orange marmalade and Italian dressing. After 30 minutes, check the chicken and brush with the dressing mix. After 1 hour, refresh the coals. Check internal temperature in the deepest parts of the thigh and the breast. The temperature should be at least 165 degrees.

MATT PELTON

When you reach 165, place 20 coals on the top of the Dutch oven and remove it from the coals on the bottom. Let it cook for 10 minutes; this will crisp up the outside. Let it rest for 10 minutes away from the heat before serving.

 AT HOME: Bake in 325-degree oven with the Dutch oven lid on. When you are ready to glaze, remove the lid and turn the oven up to 400 degrees for 10 minutes.

Method
Roasting

Completion Time
2 hours

Dutch Oven Placement
**12-inch Dutch oven
Approximately 8 coals on top,
12 coals on bottom**

**TOP
PLACEMENT**

**BOTTOM
PLACEMENT**

Hibachi
SURF AND TURF

THIS RECIPE WON us the world championship. It is a great recipe that is fairly easy to do. The pot stickers are simple, and the recipe can be played with for your own tastes. Enjoy.

FOR THE MEAT:

1 (3- to 5-lb.) beef tenderloin

1 cluster king crab legs

1 lb. fresh spinach leaves

1 (8-oz.) block cream cheese

4 Tbsp. white miso paste

5 fresh asparagus sprigs, peeled and blanched

Tony Chachere's Creole Seasoning to taste

FOR THE POT STICKERS:

Ends of the tenderloin, chopped fine

2 shallot cloves, minced

¼ cup enoki mushrooms, minced

1 egg

1 Tbsp. oyster sauce

2 tsp. sesame oil

1 pkg. wonton wrappers, round

 Cut the ends off of the tenderloin, saving the center cut—about 8 inches long. Set the ends aside. Crack and peel the crab, making sure to remove any cartilage and shell fragments. Core a hole in the center of the loin. Using acetate paper, lay out the spinach leaves followed by the cream cheese, miso, and crab meat. Blanch the asparagus and lay on either side of the crab. Roll and insert the crab mix into the

channel you created with your knife in the center of the loin and then remove the acetate paper (Pull on the end while plunging the filling into the loin using the back end of a large spoon). When you are done, trim the ends of the filling so that it is flush with the ends of the meat. Roast the loin in the 12-inch Dutch oven, turning every 15 minutes until the internal temperature of the loin is 140 degrees. Let the meat relax for 10 minutes and the carry-over temperature will rise to 145. Slice into ¾-inch medallions. Drizzle with soy sauce and serve.

For the pot stickers, mince and mix all ingredients except wonton wrappers. Spoon mixture into the wonton wrappers and fold in half, crimping the ends. Steam for 20 minutes and let stand for 10 minutes. Heat up some oil in the bottom of your Dutch and lightly fry wrappers until the edges are golden.

Pork Asian Wellingtons

Pork Asian WELLINGTONS

THIS RECIPE HAS WON us several Dutch oven competitions, and it qualified us for the world championship semifinals.

2 pork tenderloins	2 oz. rice vermicelli noodles
4 Tbsp. sesame oil	3 Tbsp. oyster sauce
2 Tbsp. peanut butter	1 lime, zested and squeezed
1 tsp. turmeric	2 eggs
4 shallot cloves	1 pkg. wonton wrappers
2 garlic cloves	1 Tbsp. oil
2 oz. enoki mushrooms	Soy sauce to taste
2 oz. bean sprouts	Spray oil

Fillet the tenderloins until they are even in shape and size. Cut off the ends so they are about 8 inches long. Take the remaining pork and chop it small and set it aside. Sear the tenderloins in the sesame oil until they are browned well on all sides. Rub the pork down with the peanut butter and season with the turmeric. Place the loins in a 10-inch Dutch oven and let them roast for about 20 minutes or until the internal temperature reads 145 degrees. While the loin is cooking, chop the shallots, garlic, and mushrooms. In a bowl, stir in the sprouts and noodles. Add the oyster sauce, lime, and egg. Lay out the wonton wrappers and brush with egg so they will stay together. Layer the filling ¼ inch deep on the shell, leaving the ends free. Set the loins into the fillings and roll, tucking the ends in. Heat up oil in the bottom of a 10-inch Dutch oven. Cook and

Method
Roasting & Stewing

Completion Time
1½ hours

Dutch Oven Placement
10-inch Dutch oven
Approximately 6 coals
on top, 10 on bottom

10-inch Dutch oven
Approximately 16 coals
on bottom

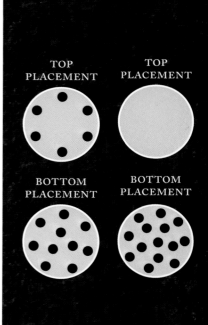

TOP PLACEMENT TOP PLACEMENT

BOTTOM PLACEMENT BOTTOM PLACEMENT

turn the Wellingtons until they are golden all around. Pat the Wellingtons dry with a paper towel. Wait for 10 minutes; then slice and serve.

With the remaining meat pieces, combine with shallots, enoki mushrooms, eggs, and soy sauce. Add this filling to remaining wonton wrappers and pinch shut at the top. Spray the dumplings with spray oil; steam for 30 minutes. Let them rest for 5 minutes and serve.

 AT HOME: Place the Dutch oven in a 325-degree oven with the lid on. Remove when the meat reaches 145 degrees. Heat up oil in a Dutch oven on your stovetop to medium-high heat. Fry the Wellingtons in the oil.

JAMBALAYA

JAMBALAYA IS A CAJUN TRADITION and is best when cooked in a Dutch oven. You can substitute the shrimp for chicken if you don't like seafood.

1 large onion, finely diced

½ cup chopped celery

1 lb. smoked sausage, chopped

1 lb. chopped ham

3 (14-oz.) cans chicken broth

2 small tomatoes, chopped

2 bay leaves

½ tsp. thyme

2 garlic cloves, chopped

4 Tbsp. shallots, finely sliced

Creole seasoning to taste

¼ cup fresh parsley, finely chopped

2 jalapeños, veined and seeded (optional)

2 cups rice

1 lb. shrimp, peeled and deveined

 Brown the onions in the bottom of the Dutch oven. Add the celery, sausage, and ham and cook until the celery is tender. Add 2½ cans of the chicken broth. Add the tomatoes, bay leaves, thyme, garlic, shallots, Creole seasoning, parsley, and jalapeños. Bring to a boil and add the rice and the shrimp. Stir them in; then do not stir again. Cover Dutch oven and let jambalaya cook for 30 minutes. Add more chicken broth as needed. Cook until the rice is tender and the broth is gone.

AT HOME: Place Dutch oven on your stovetop turned to medium heat. When you add the rice, turn the heat down to medium-low until done.

Method
Stewing

Completion Time
1½ hours

Dutch Oven Placement
12-inch Dutch oven
Approximately 16 coals
on bottom

TOP PLACEMENT

BOTTOM PLACEMENT

Method
Baking & Stewing

Completion Time
1 hour

Dutch Oven Placement
12-inch Dutch oven
Approximately 14 coals
on top, 12 coals on bottom

12-inch skillet
Approximately 16 coals on
the bottom

TOP
PLACEMENT

BOTTOM
PLACEMENT

Chicken ENCHILADAS

THESE CHICKEN ENCHILADAS are easy to make. They are great served with the Spanish Rice recipe found on page 116. I like to eat them with freshly squeezed lime, an avocado, and some fresh salsa.

1 Tbsp. oil

2 lbs. fresh chicken breasts, cut into thin strips or cubes

1 lime, squeezed

1 (4-oz.) can diced green chilies

2 garlic cloves, minced

2 Roma tomatoes, chopped

½ lb. cream cheese

Salt to taste

1 (1-lb.) pkg. corn tortillas

½ lb. queso fresco

2 (14-oz.) cans enchilada sauce (I prefer the green)

½ lb. shredded jack blend cheese

Heat oil in the bottom of a skillet. Stir the chicken into the skillet until it starts to brown slightly. Add the lime, chilies, garlic, tomatoes, cream cheese, and salt. In each tortilla, place some of the chicken mix and a strip of the queso fresco. Roll the tortilla and place in the bottom of the Dutch oven. Repeat until the Dutch oven is packed tight with rolled tortillas. Pour the enchilada sauce over the top and cover it with the jack cheese. Cover and bake for 15–20 minutes. The cheese should be completely melted and bubbly.

AT HOME: Place the Dutch oven in a 350-degree oven with the lid on.

Malibu
PORK ROLL

IHAVEN'T INCLUDED A LOT of rolled loins because they are so common in Dutch oven cooking. You can play with this recipe and roll it with almost anything. The end result is a fantastic dinner full of flavor.

1 (2- to 3-lb.) pork top loin (do not use tenderloin)

½ lb. ham, sliced thin

8 oz. cream cheese

½ lb. Swiss cheese, sliced thin

4 Tbsp. fresh parsley, chopped fine

½ tsp. garlic powder

Any all-purpose seasoning to taste

1 Tbsp. oil

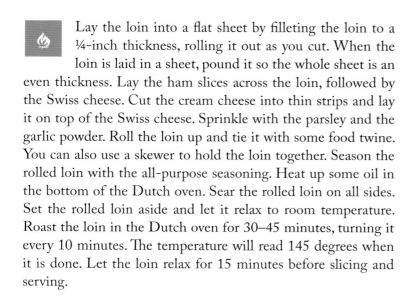

Lay the loin into a flat sheet by filleting the loin to a ¼-inch thickness, rolling it out as you cut. When the loin is laid in a sheet, pound it so the whole sheet is an even thickness. Lay the ham slices across the loin, followed by the Swiss cheese. Cut the cream cheese into thin strips and lay it on top of the Swiss cheese. Sprinkle with the parsley and the garlic powder. Roll the loin up and tie it with some food twine. You can also use a skewer to hold the loin together. Season the rolled loin with the all-purpose seasoning. Heat up some oil in the bottom of the Dutch oven. Sear the rolled loin on all sides. Set the rolled loin aside and let it relax to room temperature. Roast the loin in the Dutch oven for 30–45 minutes, turning it every 10 minutes. The temperature will read 145 degrees when it is done. Let the loin relax for 15 minutes before slicing and serving.

 AT HOME: Place the Dutch oven in a 325-degree oven with the lid on.

Method
Roasting

Completion Time
2 hours

Dutch Oven Placement
12-inch Dutch oven
Approximately 10 coals on top,
16 on bottom

TOP PLACEMENT

BOTTOM PLACEMENT

Method
Roasting

Completion Time
3–5 hours

Dutch Oven Placement
12-inch Dutch oven
Approximately 10 coals
on top, 16 on bottom

**TOP
PLACEMENT**

**BOTTOM
PLACEMENT**

Sunday
POT ROAST

THIS RECIPE REMINDS ME of Sunday dinner with family. I love the tender beef served with mashed potatoes and the roasted carrots. Make gravy with the drippings and you will have a Sunday favorite.

1 (3- to 5-lb.) 7-bone roast or similar front shoulder cut

Salt and black pepper to taste

¼ cup flour

1 Tbsp. oil

1 large onion, peeled and cut in half

8–12 full carrots, topped and peeled

4 celery sticks, left whole

FOR THE GRAVY:

¼ cup oil

¼ cup flour

1 (14-oz.) can beef broth

Drippings from the roast

 Begin by seasoning the roast on all sides with the salt and pepper. Dust the roast with the flour and pat it into the meat. Heat up 1 tablespoon oil in the bottom of the Dutch oven. Brown the meat well on both sides. Remove the roast from the Dutch oven after it is browned. Let it cool down to room temperature before returning it to the Dutch oven. Place the onions, carrots, and celery around the roast. After an hour, turn the roast and refresh the coals. Do this every hour for 3–4 hours or until the internal temperature is between 205 and 215 degrees and the meat is tender. Remove roast and let relax for 15 minutes before serving. To make the gravy: Heat the oil in the bottom of the Dutch oven.

Slowly whisk in the flour until it is coated well. Slowly add the beef broth and the drippings from the roast.

 AT HOME: Brown the roast in the Dutch oven on stovetop turned to medium-high heat. Place the Dutch oven with the roast in a 325-degree oven with the lid on. Make the gravy in a pan on stovetop on medium-high heat.

Chicken Parmesan

Chicken PARMESAN

THIS IS A MADE-FROM-SCRATCH version that I learned to cook from a family I met in the North Shore of Boston. It is made from fresh ingredients. If you want, you can substitute the tomatoes and herbs for a canned sauce. I use dried pasta because I don't always have time to make fresh pasta, although the difference is amazing with fresh. In this recipe, I substituted white grape juice for the white wine. Either works well, but I prefer the sweetness from the grape juice.

FOR THE PASTA:

¼ cup olive oil

1 lb. cherry tomatoes

4 garlic cloves, chopped

2 oz. fresh basil, chopped fine

1 tsp. oregano

4 tsp. sugar

½ cup white grape juice

½ lb. brown mushrooms, chopped

1 (12-oz.) box of pasta, pre-cooked, or 2 lbs. freshly made pasta

1 lemon, zested and half squeezed

FOR THE CHICKEN:

2 lbs. boneless, skinless chicken breasts

2 cups flour

1 tsp. salt

1 tsp. black pepper

2 eggs

A little milk to loosen the eggs

5 cups Italian-style bread crumbs

Oil (enough to fill skillet ⅓ full)

1 large tomato, sliced thin

1 lb. mozzarella cheese, sliced and grated

Method
Baking & Stewing

Completion Time
2 hours

Dutch Oven Placement
**12-inch Dutch oven
Approximately 14 coals
on top, 8 on bottom**

**10-inch skillet
Approximately 10 coals on
the bottom**

**TOP
PLACEMENT**

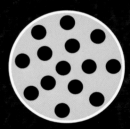

**BOTTOM
PLACEMENT**

 In the 12-inch Dutch oven, place the olive oil, tomatoes, garlic, basil, and oregano. Bake for 30 minutes. Add the sugar, grape juice, mushrooms, and the pasta. Stir it well and remove it from the heat. Remove any fat tissue from the breasts and make the breasts the same thickness if possible. Dust the breasts completely in flour and set them on a plate. In a bowl, mix the salt, pepper, eggs, and milk. Whip mixture until frothy. On a plate, dump the bread crumbs. Dip the breasts in the eggs and roll them in the bread crumbs. Set them on a plate. Heat up some oil in the skillet. Fry the breasts one at a time until lightly golden on both sides. Pat them dry with a paper towel. Set them on top of the pasta. Place the tomato slices on top of chicken breasts followed by some mozzarella cheese. Sprinkle the remaining mozzarella on the top of the whole dish. Bake for 30–40 minutes. The chicken breasts should reach a temperature of 165 degrees. Remove from the heat. Let it rest for 10 minutes before serving.

AT HOME: Use the skillet on the stovetop turned to medium-high heat. Place the Dutch oven in a 350-degree oven with the lid on.

Chapter ELEVEN

SIDE DISHES

WHAT GOOD IS A GREAT main dish if it's not accompanied by a superb side dish? I have included some of my favorite side dishes in this chapter. The recipes can be played with to suit your tastes. I hope you enjoy them.

Method
Baking

Completion Time
1½ hours

Dutch Oven Placement
12-inch Dutch oven
Approximately 14 coals
on top, 10 on bottom

TOP PLACEMENT

BOTTOM PLACEMENT

Old-Style MAC AND CHEESE

MAC AND CHEESE IS AN AMERICAN classic developed in colonial times. This recipe is greatly different from the instant style we are so accustomed to. I love the rich and creamy texture and flavor. It goes well with almost every meat dish.

8 oz. elbow macaroni	1 egg, whipped
4 Tbsp. butter	4 oz. cream cheese, Velveeta, or similar processed cheese
4 Tbsp. flour	
2½ cups milk	12 oz. shredded cheddar cheese
1 tsp. salt	2 Tbsp. butter (optional)
Pepper to taste	¾ cup panko bread crumbs (optional)

Boil the macaroni and remove them al dente. If you cook them more, they will overcook when you bake it.

In the bottom of your Dutch oven, melt the 4 tablespoons of butter and whisk in the flour until there are no lumps. Slowly whisk in the milk, salt, and pepper. Whisk in the egg, the processed cheese, and most of the shredded cheese. Fold in the noodles. Spread the remaining shredded cheese over the top of the noodles. Optional: melt the 2 tablespoons butter into the panko and sprinkle mixture over the top of the macaroni. Bake for 20 minutes. Let it sit for 5 minutes before serving.

 AT HOME: Use the Dutch oven on the stovetop to create the cheese mix. Place the Dutch oven in a 350-degree oven with the lid on.

Potato Tot CASEROLE

I FIRST TRIED A VERSION of this at a barbecue restaurant in Kentucky. Since then I have played with it until I have come up with the recipe I like the best.

2 lbs. potato tots or southern-style hash browns	Tony Chachere's Creole Seasoning to taste
1 cup sour cream	½ lb. ham, cubed small
1 cup milk	1 lb. shredded cheddar cheese

Mix the potatoes, sour cream, and milk together in the Dutch oven. Stir in the seasoning until it tastes good to you. Fold the ham and half of the cheese into the potatoes. Cover the top with cheese. Bake for about 1 hour. The cheese should all be melted and starting to brown.

AT HOME: Place the Dutch oven in a 350-degree oven with the lid on.

Method
Baking

Completion Time
1½ hours

Dutch Oven Placement
12-inch Dutch oven
Approximately 12 coals
on top, 16 on bottom

TOP
PLACEMENT

BOTTOM
PLACEMENT

Perfect Mashed Potatoes

Perfect Mashed
POTATOES

I KNOW WHAT YOU'RE THINKING. Why would anybody need instructions for cooking mashed potatoes? I was in this camp for a long time. But after years of playing around with the recipe, I have found what works best. If you want to make loaded mashed potatoes, replace the cream with sour cream and add bacon bits, shredded cheddar cheese, and fresh chives.

1½ lbs. large russet potatoes	1 tsp. pepper
1½ lbs. small red potatoes	¼ cup cream
2 tsp. salt	½ cup milk
1 Tbsp. sea salt	½ tsp. paprika
4 Tbsp. butter	2 tsp. sugar

 Begin by skinning the russet potatoes and washing the red potatoes. Cut them into large chunks. Place them in the Dutch oven and cover them with water and add the table salt. Boil the potatoes until they are tender. Strain them. until they are no longer dripping. Mash them with a masher until they are starting to smooth. Add the remaining ingredients. Stir and mash until you have the consistency you want.

AT HOME: Cook them on your stovetop set to medium-high heat.

Method
Stewing

Completion Time
1 hour

Dutch Oven Placement
12-inch Dutch oven
Approximately 16 coals
on bottom

**TOP
PLACEMENT**

**BOTTOM
PLACEMENT**

Method
Stewing

Completion Time
1 hour

Dutch Oven Placement
12-inch Dutch oven
Approximately 16 coals on
the bottom

TOP PLACEMENT

BOTTOM PLACEMENT

Chuckwagon-Style BEANS

I COULD NOT DO A RECIPE BOOK without including a Dutch oven recipe for beans. This is my favorite. It is great with pork dishes, and it is even better the next day.

1 lb. smoked sausage, cut into small pieces

4 (14-oz.) cans pinto beans, drained and rinsed

3 bay leaves

¼ cup honey

¼ cup barbecue sauce

2 (14-oz.) cans chicken broth

¼ cup brown sugar

4 Tbsp. cider vinegar

1 (4-oz.) can diced green chilies (use jalapeños if you like more kick)

Salt to taste

 Brown the sausage in the Dutch oven. Put in the remaining ingredients and simmer covered for 45 minutes. Add liquid if necessary. Be sure to stir every few minutes and run a spatula along the bottom to keep it from sticking and burning.

AT HOME: Place Dutch oven on stovetop turned to medium-low heat.

Cheesy
VEGGIES

YOU CAN USE THIS RECIPE for any type of veggie. I like to use it with broccoli and cauliflower the best. It is a simple way for a creamy cheese sauce that will keep the veggies crisp and nice.

4 Tbsp. butter	2 Tbsp. vinegar
4 Tbsp. flour	1 egg, whipped
2 cups milk	8 oz. shredded cheese
1 tsp. salt	1 lb. vegetables of choice

In Dutch oven, heat up the butter and whisk in the flour a little at a time until the flour is completely coated with butter. Slowly stir in the milk, salt, and vinegar. Bring mixture to a boil; it should thicken. Slowly stir in the egg and the cheese. Fold in the veggies and cover the Dutch oven. Let it simmer for 10–15 minutes.

AT HOME: Place Dutch oven on your stovetop set to medium-high heat.

Method
Stewing

Completion Time
30 minutes

Dutch Oven Placement
10-inch Dutch oven Approximately 12 coals on the bottom

TOP PLACEMENT

BOTTOM PLACEMENT

Method
Stewing

Completion Time
1 hour

Dutch Oven Placement
**2 (10-inch) Dutch ovens
Approximately 12 coals on
the bottom**

TOP PLACEMENT

BOTTOM PLACEMENT

Awesome
NACHOS

I KNOW NACHOS ARE NOT SOMETHING you think about when it comes to Dutch oven cooking. To the naysayers: don't mock it until you've tried it! Nachos go well as a side dish for many of the meat main courses. It also does great as a stand-alone dish.

1 lb. corn tortillas

Canola oil

Sea salt to taste for the tortillas

4 Tbsp. butter

4 Tbsp. flour

3 cups milk

2 tsp. salt

½ lb. shredded Mexican blend cheese

8 oz. Velveeta or similar processed cheese

1 cup medium salsa

 Cut the tortillas into quarters. In one Dutch oven, heat up enough oil for a shallow fry (about a third full). Separate and fry the tortillas a handful at a time until they are bubbly and crisp. Pat them dry with a paper towel and salt them with the sea salt. Set them aside. Melt the butter in the bottom of the other Dutch oven. Whisk in the flour a little at a time until it is all coated with butter. Slowly stir in the milk and table salt. Bring it to a boil. Slowly stir in the cheeses, making sure that the mixture is all dissolved. Remove from the heat. Pour the salsa on top of the cheese. Cover and let it sit for 5 minutes. Fold the salsa into the cheese. Pour over the chips.

 AT HOME: Place Dutch oven on your stovetop. Use medium-high heat for the oil and medium heat for the cheese.

Southern CREAMED CORN

THIS IS NOTHING LIKE the slimy, canned stuff. It goes well with almost any meat dish.

2 Tbsp. butter

2 Tbsp. flour

²/₃ cup milk

2 tsp. sugar

1 (16-oz.) pkg. frozen sweet corn

½ pint cream

1 tsp. salt

 Melt the butter in the bottom of the Dutch oven. Whisk the flour in a little at a time until it is well coated with butter. Slowly pour in the milk and bring it to a boil. Add the sugar, corn, cream, and salt. Stir in and simmer for 15 minutes. The corn should be tender.

AT HOME: Use your stovetop turned to medium heat.

Method
Stewing

Completion Time
30 minutes

Dutch Oven Placement
10-inch Dutch oven Approximately 12 coals on the bottom

TOP PLACEMENT

BOTTOM PLACEMENT

Method
Stewing

Completion Time
1 hour

Dutch Oven Placement
10-inch Dutch oven
Approximately 10 coals on
the bottom

TOP PLACEMENT

BOTTOM PLACEMENT

Spanish RICE

THIS IS A SIMPLE RECIPE that goes well with almost any meat dish. I especially like it with the enchilada recipe on page 100. Everyone has their own variation of Spanish rice. I came up with this one after years of experimenting with the recipe.

1 small onion, chopped fine

3 Tbsp. oil

2 cups long-grain rice

4 cups chicken broth

1 (4-oz.) can diced green chilies

1 (14-oz.) can stewed tomatoes

1 tsp. salt

1 squeezed lime

 Brown the onions well in the Dutch oven with the oil. Pour the remaining ingredients in the Dutch oven. Stir everything well. Cover and let it cook without stirring until the liquid is completely gone.

AT HOME: Place Dutch oven on your stovetop turned to medium heat.

Chapter TWELVE

DESSERTS

IN THIS CHAPTER, I will have a lot of different basic recipes for you. You can mix and match flavors to create your own masterpieces. The cake recipes given are just the sponge portion of the cake. You can split the sponge and layer it with the cream cheese frosting recipe of your choice. The same goes with pies. I will provide crust and filling recipes, but the design is up to you. I hope you enjoy the creation of so many awesome desserts.

Method
Baking

Completion Time
1 hour

Dutch Oven Placement
**10-inch Dutch oven
Approximately 11 coals on
top, 10 on the bottom**

**TOP
PLACEMENT**

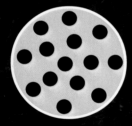

**BOTTOM
PLACEMENT**

Pie CRUST

Making a good pastry is a balance of how much you can mix it without mixing it at all. You want to cut in the fat and create layers; this will give you the flakiness you look for in a good pastry. This particular recipe works quite well, and it will yield a closed, twelve-inch pie or two, ten-inch open pies.

3 cups flour

1 tsp. salt

1½ cups shortening
(I prefer butter flavor)

1 egg, whipped

5 Tbsp. cold water (ice water is even better)

1 Tbsp. white vinegar

 Sift the flour and the salt together. Using a pastry cutter, cut the shortening into the flour until the fat is pebbled about the size of a pea. In a bowl, mix the egg, water, and vinegar. Pour the water mixture over the top of the flour mixture. Knead the dough together until it will hold together and no more. The dough works better if you have time to chill it. Roll the dough out onto floured parchment paper for easy working. Use flour between your rolling pin and the pastry if it is starting to pull. Place the pastry in a lightly oiled Dutch oven (line the Dutch oven with a parchment round and strips if you want to remove the pie). Fill the pastry and bake until the pastry is golden. (If you want to have a shiny pastry top, use an egg wash: Mix 1 egg with 2 tablespoons of water. Brush the top of the pastry before cooking.)

 AT HOME: Place the Dutch oven in a 350-degree oven without the lid.

GANACHE

THIS IS A GREAT TASTING, decorative top for a cake. We used this coating on our world-championship Dark Chocolate Cake (pg. 138).

1 cup heavy cream

10 oz. dark chocolate, cut into chunks

 In a 10-inch Dutch oven, heat up the cream. Stir the chocolate into the cream a little at a time. When the chocolate is melted, remove the Dutch oven from the heat. Let it cool down to room temperature before using. Pour over the cake and spread it with a spatula or pastry knife. Let the cake chill for the ganache to set.

AT HOME: Place Dutch oven on your stovetop with the heat turned to medium.

Method
Stewing

Completion Time
15 minutes

Dutch Oven Placement
**10-inch Dutch oven
Approximately 10 coals on
the bottom**

**TOP
PLACEMENT**

**BOTTOM
PLACEMENT**

Method
Baking

Completion Time
2 hours

Dutch Oven Placement
10-inch Dutch oven
Approximately 11 coals on
top, 10 on bottom

TOP PLACEMENT

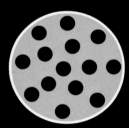

BOTTOM PLACEMENT

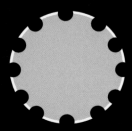

Strawberry Rhubarb
PIE

THIS IS MY FAVORITE **of any pie.** The rhubarb is a perfect balance of flavor with the strawberries.

FOR THE CRUST:

Use the Pie Crust recipe on page 118.

FOR THE FILLING:

3 cups strawberries, cut thin

2 cups rhubarb, cut thin

1½ cups sugar (substitute ¾ cup sugar with stevia for a low-sugar pie)

¼ cup instant tapioca pudding mix

¼ cup flour

 Mix all the filling ingredients together. Let it sit for 15–20 minutes. The liquid from the fruit should dissolve the sugar some. Pour the filling into the rolled out pie shell. Level and settle the fruit filling as well as possible. If you are using a full crust, be sure to vent the crust by cutting slices in the top of the pie one inch from the center to one inch from the crust.

AT HOME: Place the Dutch oven in a 350-degree oven without the lid.

Strawberry Rhubarb Pie

Method
Baking

Completion Time
1 hour

Dutch Oven Placement
**10-inch Dutch oven
Approximately 11 coals on
top, 10 on the bottom**

TOP
PLACEMENT

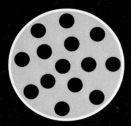

BOTTOM
PLACEMENT

Pecan
PIE

WHILE TRAVELING THROUGH the South, I fell in love with pecan pie. A lot of this love came from the fresh pecans growing all over. I have tried a number of recipes, and this is the one I like the best. It is not the healthiest recipe, but it's great for a once-in-a-while treat. For a Hawaiian twist on this, substitute macadamia nuts for the pecans.

FOR THE CRUST:

Use the Pie Crust recipe on page 118.

FOR THE FILLING:

4 eggs, slightly beaten

1 cup dark corn syrup

2/3 cup sugar

½ cup butter, melted

1 tsp. vanilla

1¼ cup chopped pecans or pecan halves

 Mix the filling ingredients together and pour into an open-faced pie shell. Bake for 35–40 minutes. You should be able to insert a knife into the center and have it come out clean.

AT HOME: Place the Dutch oven in a 350-degree oven without the lid.

Apple PIE

YOU CAN'T HAVE A SECTION FOR PIES and not include apple pie. You can use only green apples, but I like to use a mix for mine.

FOR THE CRUST:

Use the Pie Crust recipe on page 118.

FOR THE FILLING:

2 lbs. Granny Smith apples

½ lb. red apples (like Fuji)

3 Tbsp. flour

2 tsp. cinnamon (plus more, to sprinkle)

½ tsp. nutmeg

½ cup brown sugar

1 cup sugar (plus more, to sprinkle)

OPTIONAL:

Egg wash

 Slice the apples thin and add the remaining ingredients. Stir mixture well and let it stand for 10 minutes. Place into the pie shell. Cover the pie and slice to vent the top crust. (For a shiny crust, glaze the top pie crust with an egg wash.) Sprinkle with cinnamon and sugar. Bake for 30 minutes. The crust should be golden.

AT HOME: Follow the directions above. Place the Dutch oven in a 350-degree oven with the lid off.

Method
Baking

Completion Time
2 hours

Dutch Oven Placement
10-inch Dutch oven
Approximately 11 coals on top, 10 on bottom

TOP PLACEMENT

BOTTOM PLACEMENT

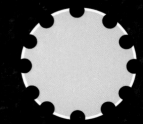

Lemon Meringue Pie

Lemon Meringue PIE

THIS IS A CLASSIC THAT WORKS very well in a Dutch oven. There is no substitute for the fresh lemons used. You can also make a key lime pie with this same recipe: use 8–10 key limes instead of the lemons.

FOR THE CRUST:

Use the Pie Crust recipe on page 118.

FOR THE FILLING:

3 Tbsp. flour

3 Tbsp. cornstarch

1½ cups sugar

½ tsp. salt

1½ cups water

3 eggs, separated

3 lemons, zested and squeezed

2 Tbsp. butter

FOR THE MERINGUE:

3 egg whites

½ tsp. vanilla

¼ tsp. cream of tartar

6 Tbsp. sugar

Begin by baking an egg-glazed, open pie shell for 15 minutes. The crust should be golden. In the bottom of a Dutch oven, mix together the flour, cornstarch, sugar, salt, and water. Whisk together well and stew it until mixture is thick and bubbly. Remove it from the heat. In a bowl, mix together the egg yolks. Gradually stir in a little of the filling to temper the eggs. Pour the eggs into the filling. Bring to a soft boil.

Method
Baking & Stewing

Completion Time
2 hours

Dutch Oven Placement
10-inch Dutch oven
Approximately 11 coals on top, 10 on bottom

TOP
PLACEMENT

BOTTOM
PLACEMENT

Remove from the heat. Stir in slowly the zest, butter, and lemon juice. Pour filling into the pie shell. For the meringue: Mix the egg whites, vanilla, and cream of tartar. Whip mixture until soft peaks form. Gradually add the sugar 1 tablespoon at a time, whipping it. The mixture should form stiff, glossy peaks, and the sugar should be dissolved. Spread over top of the warm pie filling. Bake for 15 minutes. The meringue should be starting to brown.

 AT HOME: Make the filling on the stovetop set to medium heat. Bake the crust by placing the Dutch oven in a 350 degree oven.

Amish PUMPKIN PIE

THIS RECIPE GOES WAY BACK. It is a silky custard version of pumpkin pie and definitely my favorite. In the fall, nothing is better than eating pumpkin pie with fresh whipped cream while watching a college football game.

Method
Baking

Completion Time
1½ hours

Dutch Oven Placement
**10-inch Dutch oven
Approximately 11 coals on
top, and 10 on the bottom**

FOR THE CRUST:

Use the Pie Crust recipe on page 118.

FOR THE CUSTARD:

1½ cups pureed pumpkin	¼ tsp. nutmeg
4 eggs	1 tsp. vanilla
¾ cup brown sugar	¼ tsp. ginger
¾ cup white sugar	1 cup cream
1 Tbsp. flour	½ tsp. salt
1 tsp. cinnamon	

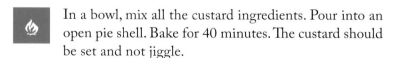 In a bowl, mix all the custard ingredients. Pour into an open pie shell. Bake for 40 minutes. The custard should be set and not jiggle.

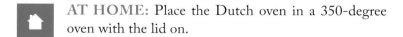 **AT HOME:** Place the Dutch oven in a 350-degree oven with the lid on.

TOP PLACEMENT

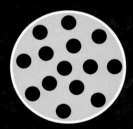

BOTTOM PLACEMENT

Method
Baking

Completion Time
1 hour

Dutch Oven Placement
10-inch Dutch oven
Approximately 11 coals on
top, 10 on the bottom

TOP PLACEMENT

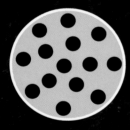

BOTTOM PLACEMENT

Apple CRISP

APPLE CRISP IS A SOUTHERN FAVORITE. Cooked in a Dutch oven, it is even better! It's hard to beat a hot crisp covered in vanilla ice cream.

FOR THE FILLING:

6 cups sliced apples

2 Tbsp. flour

1 tsp. cinnamon

½ tsp. nutmeg

½ cup brown sugar, packed

½ cup white sugar

FOR THE CRISP:

¾ cup rolled oats

¾ cup flour

½ tsp. salt

6 Tbsp. butter

 Mix the filling ingredients together. Set them in the bottom of the Dutch oven. For the crisp, mix the oats, flour, and salt together. Cut the butter in with a pastry cutter. Sprinkle the crisp over the top of the filling. Bake for 30 minutes. Let it relax for 15 minutes before serving.

AT HOME: Place the Dutch oven in a 350-degree oven with the lid on.

Apple Crisp

Berry CRISP

ΥOU CAN MAKE THIS CRISP with any combination of berries. I like to use wild, picked berries to make this one.

Method
Baking

Completion Time
1½ hours

Dutch Oven Placement
10-inch Dutch oven
Approximately 11 coals on
top, 10 on bottom

FOR THE FILLING:

5 cups mixed berries

4 Tbsp. flour

¼ cup instant tapioca pudding mix

1 tsp. lemon juice

½ cup brown sugar

1 cup white sugar

TOP PLACEMENT

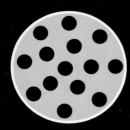

FOR THE CRISP:

¾ cup rolled oats

¾ cup flour

½ tsp. salt

6 Tbsp. butter

 Mix the filling ingredients together. Let them relax for 15 minutes. Mash the berries a little. Set filling in the bottom of the Dutch oven. Mix the oats, flour, and salt together. Cut the butter in with a pastry cutter. Sprinkle the crisp over the top of the filling. Bake for 30 minutes. Let it relax for 15 minutes before serving.

BOTTOM PLACEMENT

 AT HOME: Follow the instructions above. Place the Dutch oven in a 350-degree oven with the lid on.

Strawberry Rhubarb
CRISP

THIS IS MY FAVORITE of the crisp recipes. I love strawberry rhubarb. I hope you enjoy it!

FOR THE FILLING:

3 cups strawberries, sliced thin

3 cups rhubarb, sliced thin

2 Tbsp. flour

1 tsp. lemon juice

¼ cup instant tapioca pudding mix

½ cup brown sugar

1 cup white sugar

FOR THE CRISP:

¾ cup rolled oats

¾ cup flour

½ tsp. salt

6 Tbsp. butter

 Mix the filling ingredients together. Let them relax for 15 minutes. Set them in the bottom of the Dutch oven. Mix the oats, flour, and salt together. Cut the butter in with a pastry cutter. Sprinkle the crisp over the top of the filling. Bake for 30 minutes. Let it relax for 15 minutes before serving.

AT HOME: Follow the instructions above. Place the Dutch oven in a 350-degree oven with the lid on.

Method
Baking

Completion Time
1½ hours

Dutch Oven Placement
10-inch Dutch oven
Approximately 11 coals on top, 10 on bottom

TOP PLACEMENT

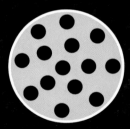

BOTTOM PLACEMENT

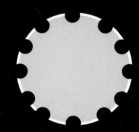

Method
Baking

Completion Time
1½ hours

Dutch Oven Placement
10-inch Dutch oven
Approximately 11 coals on
top, 10 on bottom

TOP PLACEMENT

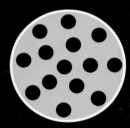

BOTTOM PLACEMENT

Fresh Peach COBBLER

THIS IS NOT YOUR SCOUTMASTER'S cobbler that so many people make. Here in Utah, we grow amazing peaches. This is so good that it's tempting to have it every day during peach season.

FOR THE PEACHES:

6–10 fresh peaches (4 cups of canned if no fresh peaches are available. If you use canned, drain the syrup and omit the remaining ingredients to the side)

¼ cup white sugar

¼ cup brown sugar

1 tsp. lemon juice

2 tsp. cornstarch

FOR THE TOPPING:

2 cups flour

¾ cup sugar

1½ tsp. baking powder

1 tsp. salt

8 Tbsp. butter

½ cup milk, warmed

Cinnamon and sugar to taste

Combine all of the ingredients for the peaches. Bake for 15 minutes in the Dutch oven. In the meantime for the topping, mix the flour, sugar, baking powder, and salt together. Cut in the butter with a pastry cutter. Slowly stir in the warm milk. Drop spoonfuls of the topping on top of the peaches. Sprinkle cinnamon and sugar on top of the cobbler.

Bake for 20 minutes. The cobbler should be browned. Let it relax for 10 minutes before serving.

 AT HOME: Place the Dutch oven in a 350-degree oven with the lid on.

Method
Baking

Completion Time
1½ hours

Dutch Oven Placement
10-inch Dutch oven
Approximately 11 coals on
top, 10 on bottom

TOP PLACEMENT

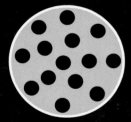

BOTTOM PLACEMENT

Fresh Berry COBBLER

Every fall, my family takes the four-wheelers into the mountains to pick wild berries. We freeze them so we can enjoy them all year. You can use a mixture of any berries to make this cobbler.

FOR THE BERRIES:

6 cups fresh or frozen mixed berries

¼ cup white sugar

¼ cup brown sugar

1 tsp. lemon juice

2 Tbsp. flour

2 tsp. cornstarch

FOR THE TOPPING:

2 cups flour

¾ cup sugar

1½ tsp. baking powder

1 tsp. salt

8 Tbsp. butter

½ cup milk, warmed

Cinnamon and sugar to taste

Combine all of the ingredients for the berries. Bake for 15 minutes in the Dutch oven. In the meantime for the topping, mix the flour, sugar, baking powder, and salt together. Cut in the butter with a pastry cutter. Slowly stir in the warm milk. Drop spoonfuls of the topping on top of the berries. Sprinkle cinnamon and sugar on top of the cobbler. Bake for 20 minutes. The cobbler should be browned. Let it relax for 10 minutes before serving.

 AT HOME: Place the Dutch oven in a 350-degree oven with the lid on.

Method
Baking

Completion Time
1½ hours

Dutch Oven Placement
10-inch Dutch oven
Approximately 11 coals on
top, 10 on bottom

TOP
PLACEMENT

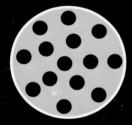

BOTTOM
PLACEMENT

Zucchini BREAD

THIS IS A BREAD THAT I adapted from my dad's recipe. I like to leave it a tiny bit gooey and eat it covered in butter.

3 eggs

2 cups sugar

3 tsp. vanilla

3 cups flour

1 tsp. salt

1 tsp. baking soda

½ tsp. baking powder

3 tsp. cinnamon

4 cups grated zucchini

4 Tbsp. butter, melted

 Mix all the ingredients together and pour into a well-greased Dutch oven. Bake for 1 hour. You should be able to stick a knife in and have it come out clean. Let it relax for 15 minutes before serving.

AT HOME: Place the Dutch oven in a 350-degree oven.

Pumpkin CAKE

THIS IS THE RECIPE THAT WE cooked for the semi-finals of the world championship. This cake works fantastic for layering. We used the Cream Cheese Frosting recipe from page 146.

¾ cup flour

½ tsp. baking powder

½ tsp. baking soda

½ tsp. ground cinnamon

½ tsp. ground cloves

¼ tsp. salt

3 large eggs

1 cup sugar

⅔ cup 100% pure pumpkin

Heath Bar topping for decoration

Cream Cheese Frosting (pg. 146)

 Mix all ingredients together thoroughly and pour into a greased 10-inch Dutch oven. Bake for 40 minutes. The cake should be set. Repeat the recipe a second time to have enough cake for 4 layers. After cakes are completely cooled, cut both cakes in half to form 4 layers. Spread a layer of the cream cheese frosting on top of the bottom layer. Repeat with remaining layers. Chill the cake before icing the top. Ice the top and decorate.

AT HOME: Place the Dutch oven in a 350-degree oven with the lid on.

Method
Baking

Completion Time
1 hour

Dutch Oven Placement
10-inch Dutch oven
Approximately 11 coals on top, 10 on bottom

TOP PLACEMENT

BOTTOM PLACEMENT

Method
Baking

Completion Time
1 hour

Dutch Oven Placement
**10-inch Dutch oven
Approximately 11 coals on
top, 10 on bottom**

TOP PLACEMENT

BOTTOM PLACEMENT

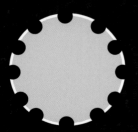

Dark Chocolate CAKE

THIS IS A SLIGHTLY MODIFIED version of my dad's recipe that he calls "crater cake." It is far and away the best and most moist cake I have ever made. This is the recipe with which we won the IDOS World Championship. We layered the cake with a strawberry Cream Cheese Frosting, which is found on page 146. We also covered it with ganache, which is found on page 119. If you want to layer the cake, do not double the recipe! Mix two separate recipes and cook them separately.

2 cups flour	3 eggs
2 cups sugar	1 cup milk
¾ cup cocoa	½ cup butter, melted
1½ tsp. baking soda	2 tsp. vanilla
1½ tsp. baking powder	1 cup boiling water
1 tsp. salt	

 Mix all the ingredients together except the water. Mix it well for several minutes. Add the boiling water and stir in well. Pour the batter into a well-greased Dutch oven. Bake for 45 minutes. The cake should be set and not jiggle. Let the cake cool down for 20 minutes before eating.

AT HOME: Follow the directions above. Place the Dutch oven in a 350-degree oven with the lid off.

Dark Chocolate Cake

Method
Baking

Completion Time
1½ hours

Dutch Oven Placement
12-inch Dutch oven
Approximately 6 coals on
top, 10 on bottom

**TOP
PLACEMENT**

**BOTTOM
PLACEMENT**

Mixed Berry PAVLOVA

THIS DESSERT ORIGINATES in New Zealand. I included this recipe at the request of many people on my Facebook page. It is a unique dessert that, oddly enough, cooks rather well in a Dutch oven.

FOR THE PAVLOVA:

3 egg whites

1 tsp. vanilla extract

2 tsp. cornstarch

½ tsp. cream of tartar

1 cup sugar

FOR THE BERRIES:

1 cup fresh or frozen berries

½ cup white sugar

2 tsp. cornstarch

FOR THE CREAM:

½ pint whipping cream

½ tsp. vanilla

½ cup powdered sugar

 For the pavlova, mix the egg whites, vanilla, cornstarch, and cream of tartar. Beat until mixture is stiff. Gradually add the sugar, beating it. Continue beating until it is thick and glossy. Place a parchment round in the bottom of your Dutch oven. Spoon the egg white mixture into the center of the parchment and work it out, creating a depression in the middle. Make sure that the mixture does not go near the edge of the pan.

Cover and bake for 1 hour. The pavlova should be firm but not brown or cracked. Remove from the Dutch oven and let it cool on a wire rack. Mix the berries, sugar, and cornstarch together. Heat up berry mixture in the Dutch oven until the sugar is dissolved. In a bowl, whip the cream, vanilla, and powdered sugar until mixture is stiff. Let the cream cool. Spoon some cream into the pavlova. Top it with the berries and serve.

 AT HOME: Place the Dutch oven in a 275-degree oven without the lid on. Heat the berries on your stovetop turned to medium heat.

Method
Baking

Completion Time
3½ hours total time

Coal Placement
**12-inch Dutch oven
Approximately 11 coals on
top, 10 on bottom**

**Camp Chef Ultimate
Dutch Oven
Approximately 16 coals on
top, 14 on bottom**

TOP PLACEMENT

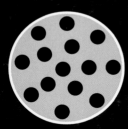

BOTTOM PLACEMENT

Lemon Poppy Seed CAKE

FEW DESSERTS BEAT a glazed, lemon poppy seed cake. If you want a bundt-type cake, use the Ultimate Dutch oven. A 10-inch Dutch oven works fine to make a cake, however.

FOR THE CAKE:

3 Tbsp. poppy seeds

¾ cup buttermilk

¼ cup milk

4 eggs

1 cup butter, softened

1¾ cup white sugar

3 cups flour

1 tsp. vanilla

2 lemons, zested and squeezed

1 tsp. baking soda

1 tsp. baking powder

FOR THE GLAZE:

1½ cups powdered sugar

1 Tbsp. butter

2 Tbsp. lemon juice

 Two hours before, mix the poppy seeds, buttermilk, and milk. Let them sit. When you're ready to bake, mix the eggs, butter, and sugar until very fluffy. Add the remaining cake ingredients and mix well. Pour into a well-greased Dutch oven. Bake for 1 hour. You should be able to stick in a knife and have it come out clean. Let the cake cool for 10 minutes before glazing. For the glaze, mix the ingredients together and spread over the cake while warm.

 AT HOME: Place the Dutch oven in a 350-degree oven with the lid on.

Banana Bread

Banana BREAD

I HAVE ALWAYS BEEN a big fan of banana bread, to the point that I would hide bananas and wait till they would get brown; my dad would make banana bread with the bananas that were too old to eat. This is a recipe I came up with after years of playing with different ideas.

3 cups flour	1 tsp. salt
¾ cup white sugar	½ tsp. nutmeg
¾ cup brown sugar	2 tsp. cinnamon
1 cup mashed bananas	½ cup butter, melted
1½ tsp. baking soda	1 cup milk
1½ tsp. baking powder	½ cup chopped pecans (optional)

 Mix all the ingredients together and pour into a well-greased Dutch oven. Bake for 1 hour. You should be able to stick a knife in and have it come out clean. Let it relax for 15 minutes before serving.

AT HOME: Place the Dutch oven in a 350-degree oven.

Method
Baking

Completion Time
1½ hours

Dutch Oven Placement
10-inch Dutch oven
Approximately 11 coals on top, 10 on bottom

TOP PLACEMENT

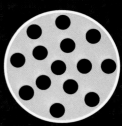

BOTTOM PLACEMENT

Cream Cheese FROSTING

THIS IS THE BASIC FROSTING I use on most of my cakes. It is easy to do, and you can create any flavor you want with it. Mix and match and come up with your own favorites.

8 oz. cream cheese, at room temperature

8 Tbsp. butter, softened

1½ tsp. vanilla

⅓ cup fresh fruit or flavoring

Powdered sugar to thicken (the more sugar, the stiffer the frosting)

In a bowl, cream together the cream cheese and the butter until smooth. Add the vanilla and the fruit; fold it into the cream. Stir in sugar a little at a time until the frosting is thick and hard to mix.

TALKING

AROUND THE COALS

Author's AFTERWORD

WHEN I SET OUT to become a good Dutch oven cook, I did not consider that one day I would become the IDOS world champion. You do not have to compete to be an accomplished cook. I compete because the competition is in my blood and it gives me a chance to blow off steam. Long before I competed, I fell in love with Dutch oven for entirely different reasons: good food, good people, and good fun. Dutch oven cooking is a culture. Organizations like the International Dutch Oven Society exist to spread the joy of cooking in a Dutch oven. When you get into cooking Dutch oven, share your passion. Look for others in your area. Look up the IDOS chapter for your area. Find events where you can share Dutch oven skills. Hundreds of Dutch oven gatherings, or DOGs, happen every summer. These gatherings are a great place to meet new friends, get new ideas, and share ideas. If you are bitten by the bug of competition, look for contests in your area. Competitions, though competitive, are a great social scene and are a fun way to meet new people.

For some, the idea of sitting around a campfire in the mountains and watching coals work magic on a Dutch oven is heaven on earth.

The best advice I can offer anyone getting into Dutch oven cooking is to be patient and have fun. You are going to burn food on occasion. Sometimes recipes will not work out as expected. Sometimes you will open a Dutch oven and the wind will blow ashes into your pot. It happens, but it is all part of the experience. The rewards include watching everything come together as it should, the smell of the food cooking in pristine mountain air, and the gasp of hungry people anticipating your food. I wish you luck on your journey. I hope that I have been able to help you to overcome the obstacles that you may have encountered. I hope that you enjoy my recipes. I hope to see you on the trail somewhere, to shake your hand, and to share more of my passion for Dutch oven cooking!

For help and information on Dutch oven cooking,
contact the International Dutch Oven Society at

WWW.IDOS.COM

Index

About
THE AUTHOR

Matt Pelton grew up in central Utah where he learned the art of Dutch oven cooking. He brought his passion with him on a two-year mission to Boston for the Church of Jesus Christ of Latter-day Saints; he packed his 10-inch Dutch oven in his suitcase. At every opportunity, he learned to cook food from the many cultures in the Boston area. When he returned home, he met and married his wife of 14 years, Katie. They have three wonderful children: Megan, age 12; Tristan, age 10; and Braxton, age 5. Matt has published two previous books: *From Mountaintop to Tabletop* and *The Cast Iron Chef.* Matt was bitten by the bug of competitive cooking and has competed in the Kansas City Barbecue Society pro-division barbecue competitions. He also competes in the International Dutch Oven Society's advanced cooking circuit where he and his cooking partner, Doug Martin, won the 2012 IDOS World Championship. Matt travels around the West competing and teaching Dutch oven classes.